EFFECTIVE EARLY
YEARS EDUCATION

EFFECTIVE EARLY YEARS EDUCATION

TEACHING YOUNG CHILDREN

**Anne Edwards and
Peter Knight**

Open University Press
Buckingham · Philadelphia

Open University Press
Celtic Court
22 Ballmoor
Buckingham
MK18 1XW

email: enquiries@openup.co.uk
world wide web: www.openup.co.uk

and
325 Chestnut Street
Philadelphia, PA 19106, USA

First Published 1994
Reprinted 1996, 1997, 2000, 2001

A catalogue record of this book is available from the British Library

ISBN   0 335 19189 4 (hbk)   0 335 19188 6 (pbk)

Library of Congress Cataloging-in-Publication Data
Edwards, Anne, 1946–
    Effective early years education : teaching young children / Anne
Edwards & Peter Knight.
        p.   cm.
    Includes bibliographical references and index.
    ISBN 0–335–19189–4   ISBN 0–335–19188–6 (pbk.)
    1. Early childhood education.   2. Early childhood education—
Curricula.   I. Knight, Peter, 1950–   . II. Title.
LB1139.23.E37   1994
372.21—dc20   94–28083
                                                                    CIP

Typeset by Graphicraft Limited, Hong Kong
Printed in Great Britain by St Edmundsbury Press Ltd,
Bury St Edmunds, Suffolk

CONTENTS

PREFACE

Much good work has been done on early years education, so why did we want to add to it? The national curriculum was a catalyst, since it redefined the content of infant education and showed signs of influencing the education of the under-fives. On that ground alone, we saw that earlier books needed to be supplanted by something that had the national curriculum very much in mind.

We also noticed the growing concern that too few of our under-fives received educational provision, leading the National Commission on Education to call for universal nursery provision and, belatedly, to the government agreeing to the principle. We doubt whether it will be sufficient to provide more places for young children. If early years education is to live up to the startlingly bold claims that have been made for it, then we are convinced that serious attention needs to be given to the curriculum, as well as to providing more places.

We feel that this is, then, a timely point at which to re-examine a raft of assumptions about effective early years education. Too often, it seems, talk of 'effective education' has failed to ask 'effective at what?' Likewise, ideas about 'good practice' seem to have gone largely unscrutinized. This book addresses these issues.

The book has been a joint venture, with each author's drafts being subject to detailed scrutiny and redrafting. However, Anne Edwards took the lead on Chapters 1–3, 6 and 7. We each wrote half of Chapter 4 and Peter Knight took the lead on the other chapters. Our thanks to Christine Armstrong, who typed about half of the manuscript.

INTRODUCTION: EDUCATION FROM THREE TO EIGHT

Effectiveness is not a simple matter

Teaching young children is one of the most important and most difficult of educational jobs. Early years practitioners have to deal with complexities that include: the social, emotional and intellectual needs of developing children; a curriculum which has been designed for the over-fives with little attention to the way children acquire skills and understanding; a multiplicity of potentially conflicting relationships with parents; and learning contexts which need to embrace the stability of routine and the stimulation required by young learners. Above all, early years specialists provide the groundwork from which children learn how to learn and become useful and valued adults. They do this and still keep the experience fun!

Too narrow a definition of effective practice might ignore the complexity that we have attempted to set out. Equally, any assessment of success has to take a long-term view, as so much of early years education has to be taken up with learning how to learn in educational settings. A major, and demanding, feature of early years practice is the sustaining of children's enthusiasm and energy while guiding them into ways of behaving and thinking that best suit the demands of later life. Nurseries and schools may differ slightly in the ways in which these demands are interpreted. Even before the most recent reforms, schooling was always run on a relatively tight agenda. Preschool provision has had, and may still maintain, much more freedom. But even here practitioners have long justified their work as invaluable preparation for later phases as well as being important in its own right.

Practitioner effectiveness can therefore be found in the ability to unravel the complexities we have outlined, to recognize how children might interpret them, to see the potential for adult action within them, to assess the value positions that underpin them, and to have the confidence and information necessary to reinterpret and reassess previous readings of these multifaceted situations. Effectiveness is evident in the intelligent action of the informed, reflecting practitioner who recognizes the complexity of early years work. The most effective practitioners we have known have often been the most tentative. They know that their actions will have a profound effect on the children's learning, that they are the most valuable resources available to the children. Consequently, they read situations carefully before acting and constantly evaluate and reconsider their actions.

Effective learners carry out similar processes to those of their teachers. They look at what a situation demands, take action and constantly evaluate the usefulness of those actions. Of course, they do not do this alone. Education lies in the carefully timed interventions made by practitioners to develop the understanding and skills of the learner. As we shall see in later chapters, practitioner intervention can be evident in a wide variety of forms.

The major themes running through the book pick up the effectiveness of early years education from four interlinking perspectives: effective learning, effective teaching, effective curriculum analysis and effective institutional development. They interlink in a variety of ways: effective teachers are themselves effective learners; effective institutions are learning institutions; effective teaching depends on effective curriculum analysis; and effective teaching cannot occur without attention to how learners learn. These perspectives place the learner at the centre of any examination of effective education and allow us to consider learners in situations which are shaped by practitioners, curricula and the kinds of institutions children find themselves in. These four perspectives are brought together in the practice of effective early years specialists through the challenge to the 'taken for granted' that comes with informed and rigorous analysis of that practice.

Generalizations about good practice often lead to futile debate. We are not attempting to prescribe good practice. We recognize practice relates to how one likes to learn oneself, as well as to how one likes best to teach and the demands of specific situations. We do, however, offer a set of ideas that have been and are being tested in the practice of early years specialists. We believe firmly that unless the ideas presented here are tested and assessed in practice, the reader will gain little. Books like this one are but a first step. Real learning will only occur when the options examined in this text are tried out. We are indebted to the large number of early years practitioners who have helped us to develop our ideas. We have learnt a lot in the process. The relationship between informed practice and tested theory is therefore central to this text.

That relationship is also important because it helps us to see that effective education is not simply about the acceptance of received notions of good practice. Instead, effective education depends upon questioning these notions, examining them from a variety of angles and considering their relevance for the task in hand.

The language of early years practice

When we look in Chapters 3–6 at how children learn, we shall stress the importance of language to what is learnt and how it is understood. We shall discuss the need to keep meanings clear so that they can be shared and common understandings achieved. Early years practice itself would benefit from being able to share the meanings that might commonly be held by practitioners but which are frequently misunderstood by those outside the field. We shall therefore now identify some key concepts in early years practice and begin to share the meanings that will be elaborated in later chapters.

◄ *Education should be enjoyable.* Learners should get a sense of achievement when something is mastered and should feel unthreatened and effective as they move towards mastery. Play is an important element in this process.
◄ *Children construct their own understandings of what they experience.* Learning takes time. Telling does not ensure learning. Young children often have a small knowledge base on which to build.
◄ *Learning is a personal experience that usually occurs in a social context.* Teachers cannot learn for learners. Learners learn a lot from other people in a variety of ways.
◄ *The learning environment is important.* Situations both allow and limit forms of behaviour. The learning context needs to be planned carefully to ensure that it enables children to learn what they need to learn.

When we look at these key concepts, we can see that child-centred education depends on well-planned and finely paced practitioner attention and support, and that knowledge is not something that can be delivered in the curriculum van. The learning child is not randomly discovering new ideas but is actively constructing new understandings under the carefully considered guidance of a practitioner who holds clear curricular goals.

An early years curriculum?

There are a number of major questions which we attempt to address throughout this text. First, can we talk about the education of three- to eight-year-olds as a straightforward progression? If we claim we can, does that mean that provision for under-fives is becoming shaped by national curriculum demands? Sylva *et al.* (1992) found that to be a real concern among the teachers in nurseries and combined centres with whom they talked. Is the view that an under-fives curriculum is determined in the post-five curriculum inevitable? Can a fightback be successful? Alternatively, is a clear curriculum orientation in preschool provision a safeguard against a view of early years education as primarily child care? Would a curriculum orientation across the whole range of preschool provision available in the

UK undermine the professionalism and status of graduate early years teachers? Clearly, teacher unions have at times felt that nursery teachers' conditions might be seriously damaged by working alongside early years care workers. These are difficult questions that cannot be ignored if we are to shape the professional development of early years practitioners as truly professional development.

Second, does a curriculum necessarily imply that practitioners should apply subject labels to children's experiences and teach each subject separately? Or does it imply that there are ways of getting to grips with a subject that are integral to that subject (fair testing in science is an obvious example of this), and ways of organizing knowledge that are essential to future understanding and expertise? Attending to the ways of knowing and key concepts in a subject does not necessarily lead to imposing a curriculum on a child. It may simply become the basis for a way of clarifying and making sense of a child's experience to enable him or her to construct new understandings most effectively.

Finally, is a curriculum simply related to the content of academic subjects? Does educational provision actually do more than attend to the intellectual development of children? We shall be taking a broad view of the curriculum. We shall pay attention to what is often called the 'hidden curriculum' and its effect in particular on the motivation and feelings of self-worth of learners.

The value base of the national curriculum is of course important, and we hope it will be open to the scrutiny of informed practitioners as they test its efficacy in practice. In this text, we examine some of the dilemmas related to values which are caused by a nationally agreed curriculum as they impinge on decisions to be made about the involvement of parents in the education of their children.

We have taken the notion of curriculum entitlement in the statutory school years as a central concern. In one sense, effective education is the assurance that pupils will acquire the knowledge and related skills that will enable the majority of them to operate effectively as adults. Such a curriculum can only at best be a good bet. It will also convey within it the current concerns of the prevailing national decision makers. Flawed as it might be, a national curriculum exists, for England and Wales at least. It may be most effectively challenged and developed, as we have already argued, by informed practitioners who have tested it in practice.

Learning teachers in learning institutions

The picture of educational experiences that is emerging in this introduction is of a carefully planned and organized learning environment in which children engage in activities that will enable them to construct understandings and so make sense of their world. The practitioner is an important feature in that picture. She or he examines the situation and takes account of the children's perspectives and what it is the children could be and ought to be gaining from the experiences. The practitioner will have planned the context and framework for the experiences and will then have evaluated the effectiveness of that work during and after the event. During the event, minor adjustments can be made; after the event, major rethinking is sometimes necessary.

One of the problems with teaching is its unpredictability. No teaching is more prone to unpredictability than early years practice. The short concentration spans, poor self-control and low knowledge base of young children do not make for a high degree of tight practitioner control over children's learning experiences. The tentative approach of the deliberative, reflective practitioner provides, we would argue, the basis of a useful set of strategies for coping with children's expressed needs while maintaining control over the direction their learning takes.

The tentative practitioner learns from children what they, the children, know, and how they have made sense of what they know. She or he then builds on that. She or he is alert to the likelihood that children will change an activity to suit them and will learn about the children from the adjustments they try to make. The tentative practitioner will readjust activities to ensure that learning occurs. The practitioner takes some risks through this way of working, but those risks are reduced by careful watchfulness and considered examination of what and how the children are learning. [Tentative practitioners are constantly testing their assessments of children and their learning needs and are continuously learning about the children. They are usually constantly exhausted, as this is a demanding way in which to teach. But they are learning a great deal. In our picture of ideal practice, the actively learning child is supported by the actively learning teacher. /

Another dimension to teacher learning is also pursued in this text. We examine the important relationship between the professional development of practitioners and the development of the institutions in which they work. We argue that confident, effective teachers are more likely to be found in institutions which take seriously the professional development of staff. At the same time, those institutions which attend most effectively to the professional development of staff are likely to be well organized institutions which engage in long-term development planning.

Early years practice as professional activity

Early years teaching is a professional activity. Unfortunately, it is not always seen as such and it is only recently that the British government has discarded proposals to allow non-graduates to become qualified early years teachers in England and Wales.

This begs the question of what a profession is. It is often argued – mistakenly in our view – that a profession is always a body which enjoys autonomy. It follows from this argument that government moves to control the curriculum more tightly have tended to deprofessionalize teaching. This view is tempting, but it neglects the body of international evidence (Burrage and Torstendhal 1990; Torstendhal and Burrage 1990; Becher 1994) that autonomy is not the defining feature of professions. It also ignores the fact that the reality of the national curriculum has meant that teachers make a great number of decisions. It has, of course, defined the areas in which they must make those decisions. However, as we shall argue in Chapter 4, there is more to do in order to make a complete curriculum, and its shape *is* in the hands of teachers. Besides, the national curriculum is a framework, not a car-servicing manual, and it leaves teachers with many professional decisions to make. For example, they have to decide which aspects of the locality are to be woven through science, geography and history, when and how; whether these subjects are to be treated separately or in topic form; which central ideas and procedures are to be emphasized; and more besides.

Instead, we are saying that a profession is defined by a body of specialist knowledge which is beyond the lay person and which only the professionals can translate into practice. We take it for granted that there are also professional standards of devotion and behaviour, but this is also true of non-professions. It is the possession of knowledge, understanding and skill that mark out a profession. We suggest that the national curriculum has marked out an important area of that knowledge. Early years teachers are professional, since they must have mastery of a nationally endorsed curriculum. We argue that this is true of teachers of preschool children, since these children are also entitled to a broad and challenging curriculum. In Chapters 1, 2 and 6, we explain that practitioners also need professional knowledge of how to teach effectively. Early years teaching is, then, a profession because of its basis in a knowledge of curriculum and of teaching practices. The fact that these teachers also have to exercise autonomy by making many decisions enhances their professionality. Therefore, we shall be taking the view that professional activity, in the sense of a mastery of curriculum and of teaching practices, is a defining feature of effective early years education.

Of course, effective early years education is a result of teamwork, involving teachers, nursery nurses, classroom ancillaries, parents and other adults. All have decisions to make and all are involved in translating adult knowledge into childish forms. It is the teacher who has oversight of all of this and the teacher who determines what other early years workers will do. It is the teacher, then, who is clearly professional, although we are sympathetic to claims by other workers to have professional standing.

We are all too aware that both professional development and institutional development planning may need to be responsive to demands made by external forces, for example the government, the local authority and parents. Staff and institutions that are best equipped to cope with change, we shall argue, are those which see staff development and institutional improvement as interrelated and as learning processes that involve goal-setting, risk-taking, testing in practice and support. We shall argue that learning institutions support staff learning and help to produce the tentative thinking practice we have suggested.

We shall examine the contribution of action research to staff and school development specifically, but throughout the text we shall take it for granted that reflective consideration of practice is part of the repertoire of effective practitioners. We therefore do not offer a list of twenty tips for effective teaching. We are not delivering a dose of good practice for practitioners to take passively with a spoonful of sugar. We simply offer some ways of examining practice, of testing assumptions and of thinking and talking about what makes for worthwhile educational experiences for young children.

BECOMING A PUPIL

Schools create pupils

As we move through our lives, we assume and act out a variety of roles. These may include child, parent, team member, leader, service user. Each role sets some commonly agreed expectations and limits on appropriate behaviour. These expectations and limits might be met in different ways. Expectations might be exceeded but limits, usually for reasons of general welfare, should not be transgressed. Being a learner in a nursery or school setting is just one of these roles. It is a role that is assumed and enacted within a set of expectations and limits already established in the setting.

The boundaries and possibilities associated with any role need to be learnt. Some roles, for example being a service user, may be relatively open-ended. You may choose whether or not to leave a tip, to return to a restaurant, or to take the advice or materials offered. Other roles, particularly those with an important social agenda, offer less opportunity for individual interpretation of role limits. Being a prisoner would be an example of a highly restricted role. The reasons for restriction usually include personal safety and communal well-being. It is therefore useful to look at the potential of any role in terms of the opportunities or affordances for behaviour that are offered in the situation in which it is enacted.

What, then, are the agenda and opportunities that can be found in educational provision for young children? In particular, what is the school system which so warmly welcomes four- and five-year-olds actually trying to do? What impact do the purposes and practices of schooling have on what being a pupil actually means for a young child?

We shall start by looking specifically at schools, but most of the points we raise at this point can be related to other forms of provision. There have been extensive analyses of the purposes and processes of schooling, which have tended to focus on questions relating to the kind of citizen a society would wish to produce. There is therefore a tendency to see schooling in terms of a way of creating and sustaining the values and associated economic priorities of the state. For this reason, schooling as a centrally organized system usually aims at producing cooperative and law-abiding citizens who act out the values on which the state operates. The processes of schooling are organized to enable this to happen. The social curriculum that is contained in the organizational structures of schools, together with the actions that these structures allow, are the premises on which being a pupil are based and are as important as the more publicly available and usually subject-structured curriculum.

The tension between the limits for action presented by this important, if somewhat hidden agenda and the need for a caring environment in which young children are free to explore and so discover what they can do will be a feature of the discussion that follows. The tension is certainly evident in the first point in a list of underlying principles of British early childhood education presented by a group of expert practitioners and researchers in 1989. Echoing the Plowden Report (CACE 1967) they asserted: 'Early childhood is valid in itself, and is part of life, not simply a preparation for work, or for the next stage of education' (Early Years Curriculum Group 1989: 3).

It could be interpreted that the sentiments of this group are at odds with those presented by David *et al.* (1992) in their sisterly response to the UK Department of Education and Science commissioned discussion document on good primary practice (Alexander *et al.* 1992). David *et al.* (1992: 6) challenge us to ask 'whether the education we provide *all* our children is high quality, purposeful and relevant to the lives they lead now, and will have in the 21st century'. For David *et al.*, schooling – even in the early years – is to be aimed at preparation for the demands of adult life. Their argument is one of entitlement and children's rights. Nevertheless, there are social control or citizen-making implications in their 1992 state-ment. We find ourselves, however, strongly in sympathy with David *et al.* and will be arguing that the groundwork of early years education should not be underestimated. But the question 'groundwork for what?' must not be avoided. Supplementary questions can lead practitioners to consider the loss of spontaneity as a result of a national curriculum and the tension between the development of the individual child and the collective needs of the larger group. Thus tension is most evident in the choices practitioners have to make about the methods they use to help children learn.

Some early years educators may wish to distance themselves from notions of schooling as a process in which citizens are created. Debates about schooling as a means of controlling and training citizens do not easily accord with early years practice and the belief that practitioners are helping children towards personal autonomy. However, most practitioners would agree that at a personal level classroom control is important. Attempts at achieving control in early years classrooms have been well documented

(Willes 1983). Practitioners' need for control is as important in preschool provision as in the more formal school settings, and the methods of achieving control appear relatively similar across the range of educational experiences offered to young children. Such similarity is unsurprising as most educators in all of these settings would wish to sustain children's curiosity and enthusiasm while maintaining an orderly calm.

For most practitioners, the ideal young learner is someone who can cope with both the hidden and the overt curricula offered in educational settings. She or he is alert and eager to master the skills and content knowledge of the more explicit subject-based curriculum and is law-abiding and cooperative in accordance with the demands of the hidden or social curriculum. Clearly, early years practitioners do not act like horse trainers and break in the wild-eyed children who are likely to create chaos in learning environments. But they do need to ensure that children learn the terms and conditions of their roles as learners. Teachers therefore need to create in young children a sense of learner identity. This identity is based on a recognition of what being a learner in an educational setting means and the behaviour it allows.

Effective practitioners try to help children to become effective learners in educational settings. Of course, this occurs while children are learning and gaining new skills and understanding about, for example, science or storytelling. The early development of a sense of oneself as an effective learner is crucial. Effective early years practitioners, therefore, often place a major emphasis on this aspect of children's learning. They recognize that it is vital groundwork. For this reason, we too look at learner identity before we look at either how children learn or what they learn.

Developing a learner identity

Let us first examine current views on identity and their relevance to the work of adults who are working with young children. Any understanding of self or identity is bedevilled by the language used to discuss it, so we will start by clarifying the terms. Rom Harré (1983), when talking about self and identity, uses the words interchangeably and describes them as 'an organizing principle for action'. The relationship between awareness of one's identity and what one as a consequence undertakes to do is crucial in education and we shall return to it throughout this volume.

Identity or selfhood can be broken down into elements of self and varying labels can be applied to these. But the most useful way forward for those concerned with education is to look at self-concept and self-esteem and at the same time to acknowledge the importance of the interactions and contexts that help to shape these elements of identity.

A person can possess a variety of self-concepts. One might see oneself simultaneously as a deeply committed parent, a semi-detached child, a reluctant team member, a reliable leader and a demanding user of a service. One's self-concept is, on this definition, simply the way one sees oneself. No value judgements are being made. This process can be observed in schools in the way that children see themselves as fast readers and slow at sums. Academic self-concept of this kind is another well-researched area and is of particular interest to teachers because, to return to Harré's idea of identity as an organizing principle for action, we tend to work at what we find easy. Consequently, the fast reader in the example we've just given might choose to read a lot.

Self-esteem adds an interesting value dimension to self-concept. It places a value on one's assessments of oneself. It may not matter to Jim that he is an unenthusiastic team member, but it may cause him concern that his relationship with his parents is incomplete. If, as a consequence, he feels that he is failing as a child of elderly parents, then his self-esteem will be low when he thinks of himself in relation to his parents.

Low self-esteem can have two possible effects. If Jim feels that he can take actions that will remedy the situation, his low self-esteem will motivate and direct that action. If, on the other hand, he feels that nothing can be done – that the gap between where he is and where he would like to be is too wide – he will do nothing. Consequently, he will feel helpless in the situation and take no action. He may then find himself blaming his parents for the difficulties and convincing himself that actually he has fulfilled his duties as well as any child might. He will then have protected his self-esteem.

A poor self-assessment of his ability as a reluctant team member will not offer Jim the same problems. Because being an enthusiastic team member is not important to him, there is no dissatisfaction with the value he places on this element of himself and no gap between his aims and reality. As a consequence, he does not suffer from low self-esteem in this area of his life.

Self-esteem can be a useful motivator for practitioners. It can be manipulated by those adults whose opinions are valued by children in ways which can enable children to acquire the skills and understandings they will need. A wide gap between aims and reality can be bridged in small guided steps, or a small gap may be created where none exists to move a child's actions on to learning something new. Motivation is a complex and important area and we shall return to it later in this chapter.

Self-concept and self-esteem are the dimensions or elements of selfhood or identity that are of most relevance to educators. Therefore, we now need to examine the processes by which these are acquired by young children in educational settings. This brings us to the importance of the context in which self-concepts are learnt and to the interactions in which they are learnt.

Julian Barnes, writing of a leading character in his novel *Staring at the Sun*, described her as clever with some people and stupid with others. We all recognize that there are some situations which bring out the best in us and others where we feel ineffective. Different contexts elicit different elements of our selves (Honess and Edwards 1987). This is because we have gradually learnt what aspects of ourselves are encouraged or limited by certain types of situation. Interaction with other people is an important feature of most contexts and it is largely in this way that we learn what we believe that we can and can't do. Obviously, professionals who are concerned with supporting children in the early years of formal education, whether in playgroups, nurseries or infant school classes, want children to create identities in those settings that enable them to operate effectively in them. Harré's idea of identity as an organizing principle for action is again a useful reminder of the need to encourage the development of a sense of being a person who can succeed at activities in the settings for which we are responsible.

Young children are particularly susceptible to the feedback they receive on who they are and what they can do. Mead's (1934) analysis has a profound contribution to make to our understanding of how society creates the identities or people that it needs. The expectations held by society are communicated in daily interactions to the young child by what Mead termed 'significant others'. The feedback of these 'significant others' has particular importance because it is usually overladen by some emotional charge due to the child's dependency in some way on the adult. Playgroup leaders, nursery nurses and early years teachers, as well as parents, are all likely to be 'significant others' for the children they work with. Later, as a sense of his or her own identity and understanding strengthens, a child will become less dependent on immediate feedback from others but will have internalized early messages and still be directed by them.

In addition to a recognition of the power of 'significant others', Mead's work has also given us the important notion of symbolic inter-actionism. Here Mead has helped us to see that the way we interact with others and with objects in an environment is directed by the way we mentally organize that environment. For example, if an important organizational category in a social group – a family or a nursery school – were gender, a stranger would note that the group was organized along gender lines. The stranger would note that gender references were evident in conversations and that there were different expectations held of girls and boys. That a gender categorization system was at work would be evident in the inter-actions of the children and adults in that setting. We all use some form of categorization in order to make sense of all the stimuli we have to deal with daily. The categories that are most obviously present in Western Europe are gender, race, age, economic status and educational level. It is rare to find in use categories that relate to spirituality, height or magic powers. At this time and in this place they are considered relatively unimportant, though among other cultural groups that may not be the case. Mead's work is of particular relevance to child-rearers and educators, because it helps us to understand that the ways in which we highlight and categorize experience and the world around us are transmitted to the young children who are dependent on us. Important categories used by adults in school and similar settings include good (not naughty), big (and good and clever), little (too little to do X), neat (not messy), listening (not talking), kind (not selfish), liked by teacher (not ignored). They may be different from the categories used at home but are quickly learnt and put into operation. One study in nursery schools showed that children as young as four could discriminate between school and home settings and the behaviour allowed (Edwards 1984).

Kate, aged four, on her first afternoon in formal schooling, demonstrated this category system at work and the power of the hidden or social curriculum in informing it. A highly articulate and bright child, she was watched in dismay by her father who had been asked to stay with her all afternoon. She gave short responses to some teacher questions, none to several and did not communicate in any other way with children or adults. She was later outraged when her parents wondered why she hadn't spoken (and by inference indicated to her teachers the extent of her intelligence). She responded, 'I was good. I didn't hit anyone, I didn't shove anyone, I didn't even push anyone'. Kate, an exceptionally quick learner, had arrived at school prepared to cope with what she had already discerned were the important categories of pupil behaviour.

Educational settings can perhaps be seen to be providing for children a set of opportunities for certain kinds of allowable action. At school, these opportunities constitute being a pupil or pupilhood. Individual children will negotiate the boundaries of these opportunities, a fact that most exhausted class teachers will confirm! But nonetheless, children do build pictures of themselves as pupils as distinct to themselves as being a family member or a football team supporter. The self-as-pupil picture will have several elements. Eventually a major one will be the academic self-concept, which is directly related to performance on the formal curriculum whether as a fast reader or a slow completer of sums.

Opportunities and constraints within a school will help to shape academic self-concept. Equal opportunities are of particular relevance here. If, for example, the gender stereotyping of play and constructional activities are not addressed to ensure that boys and girls gain access to a broad curricular experience, then opportunities to develop concepts of 'myself as someone who makes models that work' or 'who shares information' may not be available to all children.

Adults clearly have a crucial role in creating the contexts in which self-concepts that lead children towards positive action are created. An analysis of the extent to which girls might be praised for their appearance and boys for their achievements has to be part of the way we monitor these contexts, as does an examination of the ethnocentricity of our assumptions about what makes an exciting classroom. Symbolic interactionism tells us that messages are conveyed to children through the ways we select and highlight specific aspects of their behaviour or frame and emphasize elements of the environment in which they are trying to find some sense. These messages are powerful because they signal to young children what is important and what they can do and help to create their sense of themselves as learners.

The transition between home and school

If schools are creating pupils, we can equally assume that parents are shaping their children into sons and daughters with the values and aspirations that the parents emphasize in their interactions with them. Judy Dunn's work in Cambridge in the 1980s provides a rare opportunity to examine the processes and performances of very young children in their families. She reports that children as young as two have an understanding of how others are feeling and are beginning to use the social rules operating in the family (Dunn 1988). Dunn's work shows us quite clearly that by the time they are starting school at four or five, most children are quite sophisticated social operators within their families. Both Dunn's studies and that of Tizard and Hughes (1984) of mothers and their four-year-old daughters show that children in most homes have benefited from learning-oriented conversations which are usually one-to-one exchanges.

These studies therefore show us that most of the entrants to nursery and reception classes have a sense of who they are at home and what they are allowed to do. They also have a set of implicit expectations about the attention adults are able to give them, and they are adept at operating in the role of child in the family and gaining the attention they require. Most, therefore, feel effective at home.

One of the difficulties that early years practitioners have to manage is the need to maintain children's sense of personal effectiveness while they are learning to operate in a context in which the social rules and amount of adult attention will be very different. Traditional early years practice appears to address this transition by endeavouring to create an educational environment which is domestic in character. Domesticity is evident in cushioned quiet corners, in soft drapes, in the opportunities of domestic play in the home corner and in the resourcing of, for example, mathematics- and science-based activities. We shall be looking at the domestication of the curriculum in later chapters. At this point, we wish simply to note it as a device to ease the transition between home and school.

Another technique to support the gentle creation of a sense of pupil identity was documented in reception classes by Willes (1983). Her observations of teachers and children in the early days of the child's school life led her to note that reception class teachers were engaging children in the rules, rituals and opportunities of the classroom by interacting with them as if the children were already aware of the complexity of those rules and rituals. All of us who have taught in reception classes will recall our own Joyce Grenfell performances along the lines of 'We don't do that do we?' and 'Well done, everything is cleared away now we can have a story'.

What is striking about Willes' analysis is that the processes she observes reception class teachers to be using parallel those used by parents with their very young babies. Throughout the first year of a child's life, his or her caregiver acts 'as if' the infant is making sense of the world by talking to him or her and highlighting important categories such as mummy, daddy and drink. In this way, the baby is inducted into being an active and effective actor in the context in which he or she is allowed to operate. The 'as if' behaviour of the parents is at a high level when the child is very young and decreases over the first year or so as the child is able to act and communicate for him or herself.

It appears from Willes' work that infant teachers use very similar strategies. But there is perhaps a big difference between the aims of parents and those of teachers. While the low adult–child ratio in most families allows parents to see the healthy development of a child as one in which the child's eventual independent action is a priority, the poor adult–child ratio and curricular demands in the classroom give the teacher a set of priorities which are couched in the need to control the actions of the children in their care. Here we touch on the pedagogical paradox to be managed by practitioners. This paradox can be seen as how to keep children feeling effective and actively at the centre of their own learning and at the same time amenable to the constraints that shape educational experiences. It is this paradox that takes us to an examination of how we motivate children.

The well-motivated pupil

Just how do you channel the curiosity, energy and interests of young children so that they get the curriculum to which they are entitled? While no guarantees of success are given, some understanding of pupil motivation can be helpful. As we have already hinted, an understanding of self-esteem is a good start. The self-esteem equation offered by William James (1890) provides a useful framework for examining how teachers can work with the academic self-concept element of pupil identity to give some direction to pupil performance. The key to using the equation is to remember first that we are motivated to act by a belief that we will be effective when we do act, and second that we want to maintain our self-esteem. For example, faced with an unexpected guest and only two eggs in his fridge, Jim might make an omelette rather than boiled eggs because he knows that he is fairly hopeless at boiling eggs but has been told that his omelettes are pretty good:

$$\text{Self-esteem} = \frac{\text{Success}}{\text{Pretensions (goals)}}$$

$$\text{Self-esteem} = \frac{\text{Good omelette}}{\text{Good omelette}}$$

or, in mathematical terms:

$$1 = \frac{8^*}{8^*} \quad \text{(*on a scale of 1–10 of omelette quality)}$$

In this equation, self-esteem is sustained if, on the scale of measuring that is used, success and pretensions are equal. Jim has created a situation in which his self-esteem is likely to be secure.

However, if we find ourselves in situations where success is 5 while pretensions are 10 on a scale of 1–10, self-esteem is put at risk. An example of this might be a child who has been given a twelve-piece puzzle to do alone, but finds that it is too difficult for him or her to complete. As a result, we would find the following imbalance:

$$\text{Self-esteem} = \frac{\text{Doing half the twelve-piece puzzle}}{\text{Completing the twelve-piece puzzle}}$$

Crudely, in mathematical terms, the equation becomes E = 5/10.

In order to maintain the important self-esteem balance, pretensions need to be reduced so that the equation becomes E = 5/5. One way of achieving this is for the child to opt for very simple puzzles. Failure has, in this example, led to demotivation. If, as a teacher, you want to increase learners' pretensions or goals and therefore performance, you need to increase their pretensions or aims incrementally at a pace that they can manage. On the scale of 1–10, the next set of pretensions in this example might be at 6 and be slightly more difficult puzzles than those chosen by the child after failure. With support, the learner should meet his or her pretensions. But support at this stage will be particularly important.

This equation has relevance not only for setting performance levels but also for directing learners towards performance areas. This form of direction can be managed by teachers as task planners and as 'significant others'. Practitioners can use an understanding of self-esteem in order to help them set appropriately matched tasks for children. Tasks can be designed to build on children's feelings of high esteem or confidence in specific fields. Where children lack self-esteem, teacher attention to their needs can ensure that tasks are designed in ways that do not over-face and demotivate. One aspect of matching task and child with related teacher support ought to be to ensure that children will achieve success and that the success will be recognized by the teacher, though the teacher recognition element of task-setting may decrease as children become older and distance themselves from teachers as 'significant others'. In addition, as we've already indicated, the hidden curriculum can be as powerful as the official version for setting performance agenda. Most practitioners are all too aware of the time girls can spend on making their work look pretty rather than attending to more challenging aspects.

Another closely related perspective on pupil motivation comes through an understanding of expectancy effects. In a paper poignantly entitled 'Early admission: Early labelling', Rogers (1989) used an analysis of teachers' expectations of children to describe the interactive processes through which children can live down to and thereby confirm and reinforce teachers' expectations. This process occurs in a spiral of mutually confirming interactions which have been entirely led by the initial and rapidly formed expectations held by the teachers. Rogers argued that young children are particularly susceptible to the effect of these processes of self-fulfilling prophecy. He also warned about the long-term effects, for although the impact of these interactions may not be immediately evident, it appears that they may influence the child's later motivational style. Motivational style is an interesting and developing area of study. It has close links with attribution theory, which allows an examination of motivational preferences and provides another set of frameworks through which adults can examine their own roles in motivating children to learn and to be effective in educational settings. In essence, attribution theory leads teachers to see the importance of allowing children to attribute their successes to stable controllable, changeable factors that are often within the child and their failures to unstable controllable, changeable, external causes. Attributions of this kind enable children to develop a sense of their own effectiveness and ability to control or master learning contexts.

In practical terms, this means creating a climate in which real dialogue between practitioner and child is possible and in which the child is encouraged to see what he or she can do. Adults who are aware of the importance of the attributions for success and failure that children make develop repertoires of behaviour. These can include encouraging children to attribute failure to, for example, lack of effort rather than to fixed ability, and success to the amount of effort put in, to their developing ability and to the clever strategies they chose to employ rather than to the simple nature of the task. Attribution theory is in fact both more complicated and subtle than we have presented it here. It underpins an interesting and growing field of research on motivation which picks up the learner control concerns we are outlining in this chapter and gives some indication of what adults can actually do to help create confident and effective learners.

Becoming an effective learner

We have already identified the pedagogical paradox facing early years educators in schools. The paradox can be untangled to reveal the potentially contradictory aims of leading learners through the curriculum to which they are entitled, while at the same time allowing them to develop self-motivation and a love of learning that will stay with them. It is managing this paradox that is at the centre of good early years teaching.

One way through the tangle is to draw on those understandings of self and identity that emphasize agency or effective action as a central element in identity. Charles Taylor (1977), in writing about human agency, gives advice which though not directed at early years practitioners is of relevance to all who are concerned with helping children develop effective identities. He argues that we are truly agentic or effective only to the extent to which we are able to take responsibility for our actions and, importantly, for some evaluation of those actions. In other words, effective people are those who are in control of what they do and to an extent are able to judge for themselves how well they do it. Taylor's ideas help us to link possibilities for learner self-evaluation with their own self-efficacy. This is an interesting idea in early years education, because self-evaluation implies that the learner is also aware of the learning goals that the teacher has in mind.

If, as we have already argued, a sense of identity as learner is an 'organizing principle for action' as a learner, then as teachers we need to ensure that a learner's self picture includes a sense of self as an effective learner. It is easier to feel effective at something if we know what it is we are aiming to achieve. In many ways, the national curriculum has identified the learning goals that need to be met in schools. In the day-to-day work of the teacher, these goals are broken down and fed into the demands made by the specific tasks that are set for children. We shall look at task-setting in Chapter 6.

Self-evaluating, effective pupils need to be let in on the secrets of their learning activities. What are the skills they should be acquiring or practising? What element of the task is most important? Is it mathematical accuracy or aesthetic content? Some tasks may be quite open-ended and the children may themselves be able to decide on the goals to be aimed for. The important point is that self-evaluation implies the ability to recognize goals and to monitor one's own progress towards them.

Drawing on examples of work with older primary schoolchildren, Nisbet and Shucksmith (1986) identified sets of learning strategies that enable children to become self-evaluating pupils and hence effective learners. These strategies include a recognition of the goal to be achieved, the ability to work out the appropriate action to achieve the goal, a capacity to evaluate progress towards the goal, and the right to assess whether the goal has been achieved. These strategies they clustered together as 'planfulness'. They argued that the strategies can be learnt at school. Children in nursery school trying out colour mixes or the different patterning of potato prints before actually starting to work on the final presentation provide examples of how that planfulness can be developed from the first experience of school.

Planfulness of this kind is also found in the highly successful High Scope Project in the USA. In this programme for disadvantaged inner-city preschool children, the young learners have twenty minutes of planning time in small groups with an adult in which they agree on what they will do in the next forty minutes. The activity period is then followed by ten minutes of feedback in which goals and activities are discussed. A clean-up time of fifteen minutes then takes place in which incidental teaching occurs. This is followed by small groupwork, a physical activity session and dismissal. Responsibility and self-efficacy within a tightly structured environment are key features of this programme. It is arguably development from this tight framework that accounts for the long-term success of this project.

The pattern of clear goal-setting, self-monitored action and evaluatory feedback in which children's self-evaluation plays a strong part require careful training of children and long-term expectations of results. Yet again, the early years practitioner has to self-effacingly create the groundwork for later pupil effectiveness. The evaluations of the High Scope Project (Breedlove and Schweinhart 1982) are, however, stunning and show considerable social and academic benefit for pupils in adult life. But an emphasis on self-evaluation does demand a style of teaching that includes the following features:

◀ detailed breakdown of what the task requires;
◀ sharing of process and outcomes goals with learners;
◀ well-planned resourcing so that the learners are kept on task while maintaining their own autonomy;
◀ training young learners in the need to plan and to delay outcome;
◀ listening to and working with the children's own evaluations of their work.

As 'significant others', teachers are well placed to be able to highlight the processes that underpin planfulness and aspects of self-evaluation. They can let it be known that planning and constant evaluation are what they are looking for in the actions of the young children who, under their guidance, are learning to be learners in educational settings. The emphasis on process and the acquisition of the skills needed by successful learners in order to learn means that we are not talking about seeing the curriculum as a set of simple behavioural objectives which the children work to. Quite the reverse, an emphasis on learning strategies focuses attention on the *how* of learning as much as on the *what*. Having clear goals empowers learners because they are then able to make their own strategic decisions about how they might draw on their own resources and those supplied by practitioners in order to meet the goals. As a consequence, they become self-aware learners who are developing a sense of control over their own learning.

We have been describing the beginnings of the acquisition of study skills and the strategies for managing one's own learning that are evident in the most successful adult learners. The development of learner autonomy may appear at first glance to be at odds with the control needs perceived by early years practitioners and discussed earlier in this chapter. But in the ideas we are presenting, practitioner control is still strong and the demands of the curriculum are a feature of educational settings.

The success of practitioner control depends on a good match between the child and the learning task and carefully paced practitioner support. Matching can be seen in the motivational terms used in our examination of self-esteem in this chapter and in cognitive and curriculum terms in our examination of learning in the next chapter and in relation to classroom organization in Chapter 6. That the motivational and learning elements of a child's experience cannot be separated is evident in our reminder that at the centre of a child's sense of who she or he is, is a sense of what he or she can do. As a consequence, children will attempt to do what they can do best, whether that be as an effective learner in mathematics or as an effective disruptive at the sand tray!

Points for reflection

1 Look carefully at the learning contexts provided for children. What messages do they carry about race, gender and the world of work?
2 What do you think are the differences between a school identity and a home identity for a group of children you know? You may want to read Chapter 7 while you consider these issues.

Further reading

Further information on self-concept and self-esteem in educational settings can be found in the work of R.B. Burns (1982). Michael Apple (1982) has written extensively on schooling and social control. Valerie Walkerdine raises some very interesting points on social control and early education in a chapter on child development and early years education in Henriques *et al.* (1984). David Hartley (1993) offers some useful challenges to early years practice in his examination of nursery schoolings and bureaucracy. In relation to the chapter you have just read, he offers the now widely recognized view that training in self-control and self-monitoring are current bases for the maintenance of existing social order.

CHILDREN'S LEARNING

We are all teachers

The importance of language to thinking and learning will be a feature of this chapter. Yet language lets us down before we even start to discuss its relevance to the way that children take on understandings of the curricula they are offered. The English language forces us to separate learning from teaching with considerable consequences for the way we conceptualize and indeed research these activities. How much more sensible to use the direct translation from the Welsh of, for example, 'she learnt me to read'. This far more closely captures the interpretation of teaching and learning that ought to be at the centre of good teaching/learning. That interpretation can be seen both in one-to-one teacher–pupil interactions and in the wide variety of strategies employed by teachers to ensure that children are getting the learning experiences they need.

We will be tracing a theme of learning as apprenticeship. An apprenticeship view of teaching/learning is premised first on the belief that teachers have expertise and that expertise needs to be passed on, and second on the view that learners need to move gradually towards independent mastery or demonstrations of their newly acquired skills and understandings. A picture of teaching and learning as apprenticeship therefore recognizes the important role of teacher as expert, of child as active learner and of a set of learning goals to be achieved. It also acknowledges that mastery, or the ability to work without teacher support, may take time to achieve and that skills and knowledge are to be acquired incrementally with time for practice.

The framework for learning that we have just given can apply to any age and to most areas of study. But five-year-olds are very different from fifteen-year-olds and from fifty-year-olds. Young children have less information on which to build new understandings and their strategies for organizing and holding information are less well developed. They are immature thinkers and learners who need to be treated differently from older learners, who will in turn have equivalent but different difficulties when it comes to learning. Nevertheless, the apprenticeship view of learning is not simply the current best bet framework for starting an analysis of teaching and learning; it also fits well with the agreed curriculum targets that make up curriculum entitlement. Curriculum targets provide the learning goals on which mastery should be demonstrated and help define the areas of adult expertise to be highlighted by teachers in their work with pupils. There may be entirely appropriate debate about the content and sequential form of the English and Welsh national curriculum. But we believe that the notion of entitlement that underpins the emergence of agreed curricula in England and Wales and elsewhere is more difficult to criticize.

A major concern voiced by early years practitioners in the UK as a result of national curriculum targets is that the curriculum offered to younger children could become a diluted form of that offered to older ones and that children's experiences will be limited to a set curriculum. While, hopefully, these fears have proved to be largely unfounded, there is still an unresolved language problem in provision for the early years. The problem lies in the use of 'pre' as in preschool. In the preschool we are told that we find pre-literacy and pre-numeracy activities occurring. These definitions lead the activities to be seen as not quite reading and not quite number, and to the consequent assumption that there is a disjunction between preschool and school, where the real curriculum starts. This disjunction is tempered slightly by activities in preschool settings which are designed to prepare leavers for school. But these activities are usually seen as bridging the divide between the phases of experience.

Yet if the learning opportunities offered to children aged three to five are worthwhile, they ought to be, to repeat the words of David *et al.* (1992: 6), 'high quality, purposeful and relevant to the lives they live now, and will have in the 21st Century'. The national curriculum of England and Wales would certainly at least claim to meet those criteria. Consequently, if the learning opportunities offered to three- to five-year-olds are successful in matching David and co-workers' criteria, there *should* be little disjunction. The skills and understanding that are being developed in high-quality, educationally focused nursery provision might be seen as a drawing upon and building up of children's relevant competencies in ways that eventually enable a match on their own terms to the expectations of national curriculum focused classrooms in the first years of formal schooling.

Wood (1986) makes a useful yet broad distinction between the under-fives and over-fives: the attention of the younger children has to be *captured*, whereas the older children are *recruited* to tasks. Clearly, there is a curriculum to which both groups of children are directed but the work of practitioners differs. This leads us to recognize and sympathize with the enormously demanding role of the reception class teacher as she or he manages the transition from capture to recruitment in children's approaches to tasks.

Penny Munn (1992), using her detailed observations of nursery workers and young learners in educationally focused nurseries in the Strathclyde region of Scotland, has shown how adults carefully support and sustain children's experiences in nurseries to highlight the features of the experience they as experts consider to be relevant to the children's needs. In other words, they appear to operate with curricula, whether they are serving out vegetables at lunch-time, helping a child to dress after a rest or talking with a child who is completing a puzzle. These children, far from developing pre-literacy or pre-numeracy skills, are engaging with the challenges of literacy and early numeracy within a familiar and goal-directed context which allows them to work slowly and safely towards agreed understandings.

The adults whom Munn observed working successfully with children were not operating an apprenticeship model of overt adult demonstration and child imitation. Rather, they were largely engaged in short conversations in which the children were listened to and taken seriously. The children's thinking and ways of experiencing were taken one step further in supportive conversations in which the lead could be taken by either party. An apprenticeship model may operate in different forms, but it has at its centre a view of teaching and learning that recognizes the expertise and goals of the person responsible for the teaching element of the interaction. This is what successful parenting is also premised upon.

In the discussion of learning that follows, we will not therefore distinguish to any great extent between the formally agreed curricula found in statutory schooling and the more informally derived curricula evident in much preschool provision. We shall simply assume that adults have learning goals for the children in their care and that these are often long-term goals.

What are we teaching?

Chapters 4 and 5 examine the details of subject knowledge, how subjects are organized and how ways of knowing subjects are central to our grasp of subject knowledge. In this chapter, we simply indicate in general terms what makes up the knowledge structures we want children to acquire if they are to operate effectively as adults.

Writing some time ago about the structure of subjects, Bruner (1960) talked of the integrity of each subject. This he related to the key concepts and skills of enquiry that are essential to a subject. These key concepts for older children might include trade or state in history, state or medium in science and medium or colour in art. The key concepts are categories into which we can organize our knowledge of the subject and without which we couldn't operate in that subject. We can already see from the examples just given that a simple word association across subject boundaries would have variable success in matching meanings. Skills of enquiry or ways of acquiring and testing subject knowledge also differ and are exemplified in, for example, the emphasis on the fair testing of hypotheses in science but not in history in primary classrooms.

While there are enormous advantages in being able to draw on expertise in several subjects to make creative connections, that expertise has first to be acquired. We are therefore arguing that once there is curricular clarity about the key concepts of a subject and ways of knowing that subject, teachers are better able to highlight and shape important features of the learning experiences offered to children and to start to develop subject-discrete bodies of knowledge. Once the groundwork in learning has been done and knowledge is organized in relatively simple subject-based categorizations, creative connections may be more easily made and tested. We are, of course, aware that we are begging questions of the validity of subject boundaries. But we think that the questioning of boundaries is likely to be more successful when it is informed by an understanding of their limitations than by the occasionally successful intuitive leap. Again we take these points further in Chapters 4 and 5.

We have just used the word 'groundwork' quite deliberately to emphasize the important role of early years practitioners in the initial formation of knowledge categories and skills of enquiry. Quite clearly, we are suggesting that any notion of the early years curriculum as a seamless web of experience is counterproductive to empowering children to operate effectively with commonly accepted categorizations of public knowledge. *We are not, however, arguing that these knowledge categories should be acquired in ways that appear irrelevant, demotivating and alien to young children.* We return once again to the pedagogical paradox we discussed in Chapter 2. The challenge for early years teachers is how to help children to begin to organize their experiences of the world in ways that will enable them to build on those categories as they acquire more knowledge and become more sophisticated learners, and to do that without damaging the curiosity, confidence and fun that young children can gain as they try to make sense of the world about them.

All children are learners

While sheep grow fleeces to enable themselves to adapt to a chilly climate, we humans adapt more intelligently to our environment. We learn how to act upon it so that we can survive within it. We become better at these actions as we become more mature thinkers, but without the ability to think and learn we would be unable to survive. Just note the ways in which toddlers try to manipulate their parents. Learning is therefore the mechanism we use to allow ourselves to gain some kind of control or mastery over our environment.

We actually know very little about the mechanisms and processes of children's learning. We can only work with the 'best guesses' presented to us by research psychologists. These guesses are usually validated as much as they can be by supporting evidence of children's behaviour and knowledge structures. But because they are recognized as 'best guesses', they are even more open to the possibility of disproof than other scientific propositions. One consequence of this lack of certainty is the amount of fascinating research that has been carried out on what young children can do and how they understand events, as developmental psychologists attempt to build up a detailed picture of the young thinker.

Educators in school or preschool settings will, of course, want to apply the relevance test to psychological research. The test is quite simple. It requires an affirmative to the question: 'Is this information likely to help me develop the way I work with children?' Research which has itself asked educational questions is likely to be of most relevance. But we do urge an open mind. Relevance is not always immediately apparent.

Piagetian research – both Piaget's own work and the studies of others who have explored his frameworks – does not always ask educational questions, but it does provide some useful starting points for an exploration of current 'best guesses' of how children think and learn. Piaget himself did not ask an educational question. His preoccupation was a more esoteric or arguably fundamental enquiry into how knowledge develops. His work had a particular, but not exclusive, focus on logico-mathematical thought. His research question begged the educational questions of 'What is it that children should learn?' and 'What can I do as a teacher to assist that learning?' Nevertheless, his work has produced a broad framework for an understanding of the processes of how children think and learn which has yet to be bettered.

These processes carry the indigestible names of assimilation and accommodation. *Assimilation* occurs when information is taken in by the mind without requiring any adjustment of the knowledge categories that already exist. This can happen for two reasons. First, the information can be undemanding because you already know it and have categorized it; for example Rome is the capital of Italy. The second form is when the information is so complex that you cannot begin to categorize; for example, for at least one of the authors this would be the relative positions of Rome and Avignon in the Catholic Church during the Middle Ages. In the second example, the mental category system of one of the authors cannot make connections with enough of the new information to begin to categorize it in any way that makes sense. There has therefore been an inappropriate match between the new information and the learner. This poor match is more of a problem in the second example than in the first, for although the information that Rome is the capital of Italy is not new information, it at least allows the recipient to revisit, revise and check an existing category. There are, however, some advantages to the second example. The recipient now knows that Rome and Avignon were linked in some flux of power or position in the Catholic Church in the Middle Ages. She or he can do little yet with the information, but will perhaps become more alert to related topics and eventually begin to build up a picture of the period.

Young children engage in assimilation much more of the time than do older learners because young minds usually have a less developed category system with which connections can be made. Imaginative play is where we see a great deal of assimilation. Children act on the world by turning the world to their own purposes (e.g. using a flower pot as a hat or a cardboard tube as a telescope). In this kind of play, they are becoming familiar with objects and expectations without actually taking on board their full functions. This can be seen in adults too as they, for example, play with new photographic equipment to become familiar with it before actually using it. Plenty of opportunity for play that allows children to become familiar with the tools, materials and language they will need has long been a feature of good early years provision. But you will have noticed how the curriculum has crept in with the mention of the *relevance* of tools, materials and language. Relevance is measured in relation to wider curricular goals.

Accommodation is what happens when the mind gets into gear and adapts existing categories or ways of organizing information to fit in new information. In some cases, it may be a question of simply extending an existing category, for example by adding Rome to the list of capital cities you already know. On the other hand, it may be a question of adjusting existing categories. For example, you may have a category 'big cities' which has to be adjusted once the idea of capital cities as a category is introduced. Consequently, Paris, London and Rome are placed in the capital city subcategory of your big cities category. What happens when Reykjavik is introduced as a capital but not a big city indicates just how complex a process is the categorization of knowledge.

The teacher's role in sequencing learning experiences and in supporting the accommodation process of the learner is important and always depends upon the success with which a teacher can diagnose how a learner is understanding or categorizing the information already held. For information to be accommodated successfully, new information needs to be at a level of novelty which ensures that connections to existing category structures can be made in meaningful ways. Often teacher help is necessary in, for example, naming and identifying the new or adjusted categories. This is one simple view of the match of experience and learner. We shall return to both match and the importance of language in categorizing knowledge a little later in this chapter.

A child playing with wet sand – sometimes simply enjoying the sensation of damp roughness, sometimes repeating rituals of chugging a bulldozer along smooth pathways, sometimes making tunnels and beginning to get a sense of how long a tunnel can be in proportion to its width and the amount of sand around it – is not simply either assimilating or accommodating. She or he is doing each in turn. Assimilation and accommodation are each occurring in sequence. Accommodation occurs as the child tries to find a way of balancing external stimuli with internal ways of organizing knowledge. It is this constant but shifting balance which typifies learning and the active minds of children who are testing stimuli and trying to make sense of them.

The definitions can be enormously helpful to teachers because they help us to see the value of imaginative play (usually mainly assimilation) and problem-solving play (often allowing and encouraging more accommodation). Once we add the learners' need to label knowledge categories to Piaget's own concerns with the actual learning processes, we can begin to see the importance of the role of teachers in assisting the organization of knowledge.

Table 3.1   Piagetian stages of development (ways of acting on the world)

Stage	Description
I	Sensori-motor
II	Pre-operational
	(a) pre-conceptual
	(b) intuitive
III	Concrete operations
IV	Formal operations

Piaget's description of developmental stages (see Table 3.1) is more open to critique than his analysis of the learning processes. The stages become a dangerous framework if ages are attached to them and the curriculum is pinned to age-related ways of acting in the world. Working on science education, Shayer and Adey (1981) have shown that, for example, only 30 per cent of nine-year-olds and 75 per cent of fourteen-year-olds have full use of concrete operations. They also note that only 30 per cent of adults make use of formal operations.

Piaget's breakdown into stages of the ways in which people operate on the world as they try to make sense of it (Table 3.1) does have a very useful purpose. It reminds us that young children do deal with events in a qualitatively different way from older learners. They are much more likely to have to resort to intuition simply because they cannot always hold in their minds two separate pieces of information and then connect them. The minds of children at this stage can be likened to a slide presentation in which discrete images are shown in turn. Only later does life become a video. Piaget's analysis therefore alerts us to the need to find out how the child is operating on the world and to create learning experiences which enable that child to move towards the next developmental stage of operation.

So children may be always learning, but how can we be sure that they are learning what we want them to learn in the most efficient way? How do we direct, structure, sequence and support their learning?

Learners need teachers

The statement that learners need teachers is more open to question than the assertion that we are always learning. Were it presented as a question, the answer would have to be 'yes but only some of the time'. The casual response belies the complexity on which it rests. It is this complexity which we shall now tease out while paying particular attention to the organization and structuring of contact between practitioners and learners.

We shall start with clarifying some of the dimensions, variables or demands that teachers in educational settings have to take into account when they support and guide children's learning. We are certainly not claiming that educating others is easy. We are also not suggesting that it can be broken down into a set of mechanical operations which once learnt can be applied in all situations. Teaching is above all led by sensitivity to the state of the learner. A learner's state will include motivations, confidence and existing understandings. Formal teaching is ultimately the making of appropriate purposeful interventions. These interventions can be exciting introductions, encouraging revisions, challenges, praise and distant monitoring.

Central to the statement that learners need teachers is the idea that learning is goal-directed. It is certainly the aim of all teachers that learners learn something worthwhile! We have already argued that children in informal early years settings are learning how to operate independently within the boundaries of behaviour accepted in their communities. They are learning to become people who will fit in and operate effectively. Once they meet the formal curriculum in school, learning goals simultaneously become narrower, as specified elements of a defined curriculum, and more universal, as commonly or publicly understood elements of a national curriculum. The teacher's role becomes at the same time more limited and more important to the child. Children can't acquire the national curriculum at home. Learning goals become more explicit as the school takes responsibility for delivering the curriculum to which the child is entitled.

Learning is a slow process if it is lasting learning and not simply fleetingly held. Vygotsky, writing in Russia in the 1920s and 1930s, provided a framework for teaching and learning which has stimulated a considerable amount of useful work in the last two decades on how teachers help learners. His starting point was that learning occurs on two levels or 'planes', both of which have to be experienced if learning is to take place. The first level he calls the *intermental*. This is the social level at which the learner first hears the language and perhaps experiences, alongside others, the tasks which demand repetition of the language in which the concept or idea to be learnt is carried. Understanding is hazy and rather similar to the feelings that many adult learners experience when they walk out of a lecture theatre. The analogy is apt as they too may have been immersed in a language bath of unfamiliar terms which are keys to the concepts they must acquire if they are to master the subject.

The second level he calls the *intramental*. This is the individual or personal level at which each learner tries to make sense of new knowledge and connect it clearly to what she or he already knows. The learner has to work hard here, and the support and guidance of the teacher is crucial and demands skill. To continue the lecture analogy, this stage in the learning cycle is found in the seminars and study group activities established to follow up and consolidate lectures. During the intramental stage, the learner becomes increasingly independent of the teacher. The learner takes on the concept and incorporates it into his or her repertoire of understanding and actions. The final outcome is learner mastery, which is evident in some kinds of performance.

We shall be emphasizing Vygotsky's framework because it reminds us continuously of the key features of a teaching and learning cycle:

◀ the relationship between language and concept acquisition;
◀ the shifting role of the teacher;
◀ the active engagement of the learner.

We shall now look at each of these in turn.

The relationship between language and concept acquisition

Responding to the question of whether it is the language or the idea that comes first for learners, Wells (1981: 81) stated: 'existing concepts [provide] a clue to the meanings of words heard, and words [lead] to a modification of existing concepts, with the situational context in both cases providing additional support in establishing a relationship on particular occasions'. We will see in Chapters 4 and 5 how important the careful use of language is to acquiring expertise in the subjects that make up the curriculum. Getting it right in the early years is giving the children a good start. Here we return to the point about groundwork that we made earlier in this chapter. So how do teachers organize and structure the learning cycle with language acquisition and use in mind?

The language-rich environment is certainly important. Clearly written labelling, word banks, books produced by the children and tape recorders all help to create a context in which the relationships between thought, action and language are central features. Let us for the moment take these teacher-stimulated features for granted and concentrate on what teachers can do with children. General contextual topics will be discussed more fully in Chapter 6.

We shall deal relatively quickly with the most obvious first stage of the teaching and learning cycle and language. The first stage is usually a large group activity into which key words are introduced by the teacher through perhaps talking about an experience, artefact or piece of equipment.

Children's questions and sharing of related experiences often follow, with the teacher carefully repeating the language she or he wants to be used in the next activity. It often appears to be an informal, open-ended activity, but it is in fact carefully orchestrated by the teacher to ensure that the language formats that are central to concept acquisition are repeated frequently. This is similar to Vygotsky's intermental stage.

The next stage may involve table tasks in groups of two or three (see Chapter 6 for a discussion of group structure and classroom learning). The tasks that are set for the children are carefully contrived to ensure that they use the language the teacher wants used. But of course they won't! Not without teacher help anyway. The following extract shows how a teacher structures an activity with two six-year-olds to develop their use of the language associated with dividing by two. Keep in mind Wells' description of concept acquisition as you read it.

Teacher: What did I mean when I said divide them between the two of you?
Child 1: Take them away.
Teacher: Take them away from what?
Child 2: From three and you make it into two and two.
[Teacher points to the multilink]
Teacher: Tell me about this lot and that lot.
Child 1: Well they are in twos.
Teacher: Anything else you can tell me?
Child 1: They're both reds and those are red and yellow.
Teacher: Yes – and how many are there?
Child 1: Two.
Teacher: And how many are there?
Child 2: Two, so there are four.
Child 1: Richard's and mine are the same.
Teacher: Let's tip some more out. Can you divide these between the two of you?
Child 1: You have to have them equal don't you?
[Puts them into two groups]
Child 2: I've got four and he's got four.
Teacher: How many are there altogether?
Child 2: Eight.
Teacher: I'm going to tip out a whole lot more.
Child 1: If you want one in the middle you have to get the odds don't you?
[They divide them out]
Child 1: You can't divide them the same because it's odd.
Teacher: So what are you going to do?
Child 1: You'll have to divide it by three.
Teacher: But weren't you dividing them between the two of you?
[Children try again]

Child 1: No you can't divide that Richard – that's not properly divided.

[Child 2 counts his pile]

Child 2: That won't work.

[Child 2 counts ten and child 1 counts eleven]

Teacher: What do you think you should do now?

Child 1: Take one away.

Teacher: What are you going to do with it?

Child 1: Put it in the leftovers.

You can see here how Child 1 is groping towards the language that will empower him mathematically with his use of 'odds' and 'leftovers'. You will also have noticed the teacher's intervention to keep the children on task and dividing by two and the masterly way in which she keeps them actively in charge of the task with a form of questioning which demands that they use mathematical language to explain their actions. The next stage is for them to do more of the same so that they become confident in the repeated formats of odd numbers, divide, take away and even 'leftovers'. This can be done with less teacher supervision.

Performance and written evidence come much later and may be through the incorporation of these understandings into a problem-solving task. We would argue that in most cases mathematical worksheets are mainly of value to children's learning if the aim is to speed up the response rate. They do have other advantages, not the least of which is freeing up the teacher to have the kind of interaction with small groups of children we have just discussed. And of course that is not to be discounted.

The shifting role of the teacher

The discussion of language acquisition and use has already indicated the nature of the shift. The teacher's function appears to move from leading with a large number of learners to guiding with a small number of learners, then to more distant monitoring as the learners begin to work with the language and ideas and, finally, to fairly low monitoring as the children actually use the acquired language and ideas in a variety of situations. We shall discuss this shift in terms of planning for teaching and the use of teacher time in Chapter 6. Let us now return to how this relates to Vygotsky's ideas.

What is not always obvious to onlookers in classrooms is the extent of diagnostic assessment that is going on. Practitioners are constantly assessing children's understandings and adjusting task demands to suit them. This is just another example of the way in which Vygotsky's frameworks are compatible with good educational practice. Sound assessment was the starting point for his work with children and remained central to his view of how the more expert support the learning of the less sure.

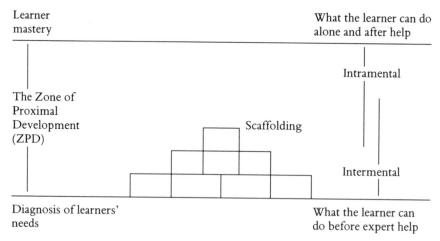

Figure 3.1   A Vygotskian framework for teaching and learning

Figure 3.1 shows in a very crude form the framework for teaching and learning that Vygotsky's writings have given us. It incorporates the 'scaffolding' that, for example, Wood (1986) has explained is supplied by the more expert teaching partner in the enterprise. You will note, in the context of the last few paragraphs, how the amount of supportive scaffolding reduces as the learner moves towards mastery.

Vygotsky's Zone of Proximal Development (ZPD) gives an interesting and very positive view of assessment and teaching. Children's ability, in Vygotskian terms, is measured by the speed at which they can move through the ZPD. This is a measure of how they master new information, rather than a simple testing of what they know. Implicit in this view is the expectation that whoever is in the teaching role will diagnose the learning needs and provide appropriate scaffolding. Clearly, this is a view of teaching and learning as a joint enterprise.

Figure 3.1 allows us to see how the teacher's role moves from heavy involvement early on to very light monitoring later. We can also see the importance of continuous assessment as decisions about structuring support are made. We'll pick up on these points again in Chapter 6 but will leave you here with the suggestion that time spent testing pupils at the mastery stage may not be the best use of the most valuable resource for learners – that is, the teacher. However, time spent assessing in order to select tasks and give appropriate support to children as they progress through their ZPDs is good use of practitioners' time.

The active engagement of the learner

One of the myths of early years education that is at last being dispelled is the idea that child-centredness and curriculum-centredness are a simple 'either/or'. We hope that our discussion of curriculum as entitlement earlier in this chapter has laid the ground for further questioning of the assumption.

We know only too well that we can take a child to the curriculum but we can't make him or her learn! The best we can do is attempt to match the task in which the curriculum is carried to the cognitive and motivational state of the child. We are using the word curriculum deliberately broadly to include not only the prescribed curriculum of the infant school but also the more flexible curriculum provided for younger children.

Thoughtful, education-minded workers in nurseries and preschool playgroups, as well as in nursery schools, have created stimulating learning contexts which attend to both the cognitive and more emotional needs of children. Ranging from safe treasure baskets for the baby who can sit, the provision of wall mirrors, sensation tables and quiet corners to sand and water opportunities, these settings have made active learning compulsory. The only way to avoid learning in these situations is to stay away! But a quick look at these settings can be misleading. The environment is not a random array of experiences in which children take the lead. The adults have made curricular decisions when setting out the materials and they carefully deploy themselves to talk with the children and to support and guide the ways in which they make sense of the world. They diagnose what the children understand and attempt to move them onwards either by allowing them to practise and demonstrate what they know or to increase their understanding by, for example, exploring another attribute common to the materials available. The joint enterprise of teaching and learning is in operation.

Once children reach statutory schooling age, the curriculum becomes less flexible and matching experience and child becomes more problematic if the child's motivational state is always to be given the consideration it should receive. We examined motivation and match in Chapter 2, so we will concentrate on the cognitive aspects here. As we stated earlier, learning is a long, slow process. We want to emphasize the word *process*, because that allows us to see that matching learning experiences to learners is no simple matter.

We shall talk in more detail about tasks and task-setting in Chapter 6, and have already mentioned the importance of both assimilative and problem-solving play and the value of visiting information even if it is not fully understood. We shall at this point simply think about the different types of tasks or experiences for learning, their purposes in the long process of learning and how we might keep children actively on task and learning.

In Fig. 3.1, you can see that the learner starts on the journey through the ZPD with a great deal of teacher support, that there is less at the midpoint and very little as the learner works towards mastery. It is therefore quite useful to think of three different types of task or experience as children take on new understandings. We are here taking it for granted that what they finally understand will be coloured or shaped by what they knew when they started.

Norman (1978) and Bennett *et al.* (1984) have used similar frameworks for explaining how tasks might differ as learners move through the cycle or process of learning. They have helped us to see that matching experience to a learner is not simply a question of introducing new information and expecting the learner to acquire it (which is what happened in the formal classrooms of yesteryear), nor of setting up novel experiences for the child to experience and act upon (which is what the critics of progressive education feared that discovery methods involved). As Desforges (1985) put it, match is a complex cognitive issue.

The three types of task or experience that can be distilled from the work of both Norman and Bennett *et al.* can be described as three stages or types of task demand aimed at a clear set of learning goals:

◄ teacher-led tasks or working alongside the teacher;
◄ teacher-structured tasks with close teacher monitoring;
◄ either practice or problem-solving tasks in which new skills or concepts are used and teacher presence is low.

These stages can be seen as a learning sequence. As the teacher's role shifts away from the child, the child as active learner takes increasing control of the tasks that are set and what is learnt from engaging in them. Our discussion of the importance of language earlier in this chapter has already indicated the need for getting the right language in use early in the task process just outlined.

If we take the sequencing of shapes as a learning outcome and thinking about a series of small tasks related to printing a piece of wrapping paper as an example, we can illustrate the task demands quite simply:

1 *Stage 1*:
    ◄ looking at wrapping paper and patterns with the teacher;
    ◄ choosing printing shapes and colours in discussion with the teacher;
    ◄ deciding on patterns in discussion with the teacher.
2 *Stage 2*:
    ◄ trying out colours and talking to other children;
    ◄ trying out shapes and talking;
    ◄ trying out combinations of shapes and talking;
    ◄ designing/testing patterns.
3 *Stage 3*:
    ◄ printing a piece of wrapping paper;
    ◄ discussing patterns with others.

All three stages are important, but Stage 2 is crucial because it is here that the transition to ownership or *internalization* (i.e. the intramental plane) occurs. The child takes control of his or her learning and is not simply producing an object to satisfy the teacher but is thinking and making decisions.

Not all opportunities for matching are as easily arranged as the example we've just given. What about the children who have not managed to sequence the shapes at Stage 2? For motivation purposes, they will be allowed to move to Stage 3 this time, but new tasks will have to be devised to scaffold their understanding of sequencing and they'll need to return to new versions of all three stages.

One of the most stunning revelations in Bennett and colleagues' (1984) study was that those seven- and eight-year-old children who were slowest at moving through these stages in mathematics were those who also had less time for consolidation and practice. The slowest learners who had most need of consolidation were the very children who were denied it because their teachers felt obliged to drive the children through the curriculum. And this was before a national curriculum was in place. Doubtless these children soon began to feel that their own learning was out of their control.

In all three stages just outlined in the printing task, children's decision making was playing a vital part. In Stage 1, they selected shapes and colours, probably from a limited array, and decided on pattern sequences. In Stage 2, they made judgements about the quality of their work and the degree to which it reached agreed goals. In Stage 3, they not only completed the task but engaged in evaluatory discussions with others. The curriculum was not being done *to* the children. Conversely, they were acquiring and using new skills and understandings and keeping their individuality. The pupil self-evaluation that was occurring in Stages 2 and 3 (discussed in Chapter 2) is an example of another important piece of groundwork that early years teachers provide. Useful learning strategies are being developed that are overtly recognized in, for example, design and technology curricula, but they are also relevant to adult learners when planning an essay or undertaking a development project in the workplace.

Learning through play

Where in all this talk of goals and curriculum lies the opportunity for play? Our response is that we would not recommend that you try to keep young children away from the opportunities for learning that play brings them. You can, if you must, take the play out of learning, but it is more difficult to take the learning out of play. If you do, however, take the play – or low-risk opportunities for trial and error – out of learning, the learner will find learning more difficult. While this holds true for adults, it becomes increasingly the case the younger the learner.

Let us nonetheless conclude this chapter by asking some quite practical questions about the relevance of play to children's learning:

1 *Do we all mean the same thing when we talk about play in early years education?* Piaget and Bruner clearly didn't. For Piaget play was a necessary activity but also a sign of immature functioning. It was evidence that the child had not grasped the common understanding of the concept

involved. Play helped the child move towards understanding as he or she acted on the object and turned it to his or her own imaginative uses. But once the child understood the functions and used them purposefully, the activity was no longer play. This is a pretty limited view of play. Bruner's definition is wider and includes both exploratory play in which children experiment, often quite purposefully, with materials, and social play in which children acquire the rules and rituals of the society to which they belong.

2 *Is play real?* Children themselves see play as an activity that is a safe place in which liberties can be taken. How familiar is the claim, 'But I was only playing!' Equally, they will assert their own control by refusing to play.

3 *Does the unreality of play mean that all play should be imaginative play?* Bruner's definition of play would lead us to say 'no'. One of us remembers well the despair of a nursery worker who, exasperated in a planning meeting, exclaimed: 'Why can't they simply see a milk carton as a milk carton! Why do we always have to turn it into something else!' A good question.

4 *How can we make the most of imaginative play?* If play is simply a route to wider understanding rather than an end in itself, the nearer we move the resources available to the real world the better. How much more valuable in a nursery setting to have a walkie-talkie system that works than one that simulates. The children making the wrapping paper in the example earlier in this chapter were not making pretend wrapping paper, but were using their imaginations and in Stage 2 playing with the design options available to them as they planned their final designs.

Teaching and learning are serious activities that need to be fun, particularly when they involve young children. Fun comes when we are in control. Children enjoy learning when they are in control of what they are doing. But that usually only occurs as a result of the work of a skilled teacher – whether parent, nursery worker or class teacher.

We therefore suggest very strongly that formal curricula do not require what are sometimes called formal teaching methods. Here again we return to the points with which we started this chapter. Our language lets us down when we talk about learning and teaching. The alternative to what are commonly regarded as formal teaching methods is not random informality but carefully structured situations in which children work with adults, other children or alone as they master the skills and concepts they need in order to function effectively.

Points for reflection

1 Do you agree with David Wood's distinction between teaching young children and older children? Does the difference between 'capture' and 'recruit' do

justice to the differences and similarities in the work of practitioners with the younger and older children in the three to eight age range?

2 Think of something that you have tried to help a group or a single child to learn. Did you go through the three stages we have just outlined? If not, what did you do? Is the three-stage model a helpful one?

Further reading

Nigel Hall and Lesley Abbott (1991) have edited a helpful book on *Play in the Primary School* which takes into account the national curriculum. Charles Desforges (1989) edited a pre-national curriculum collection on early years education which contains some useful papers. David Wood's (1988) examination of Vygotskian theory and children's thinking and learning gives the detail that is impossible to provide here.

A CURRICULUM
FOR THE EARLY YEARS

Development or learning?

In the previous chapter, we suggested that a knowledge of child development is important to educators of young children because of the need to be sensitive to how children are able to handle information. We argued at the same time that knowledge of the developing child is not the only factor to be taken into account by teachers. We talked about goal-setting and the introduction of children to wider cultural understandings. Access to an understanding of what is considered to be necessary to know in order to operate effectively is something to which children in the state system of schooling are entitled. It is this learning that educators in the state system manage. In England and Wales, they manage it by inducting children into the key understandings and skills carried by a nationally agreed curriculum. We are aware that at this point we are again begging the question of the value bases of such a curriculum. Teachers of children aged five and older by no means ignore child development, but they become more curriculum-focused as they are also responsible for seeing that children acquire the knowledge and skills that are highlighted in the national curriculum. We hope that the previous chapter has convinced you that acquiring curriculum knowledge can still be achieved in child-centred ways which draw on an understanding of child development and indeed have to be if children are to learn in any meaningful way.

The choice of emphasis between development and learning appears more problematic for those working with younger children. Clearly, professionals in this field need to recognize the capabilities and needs of developing children, but this emphasis does not mean that learning and, by implication, learning goals, are not important.

At this point, we want to distinguish between intellectual development and education. Intellectual development follows, more or less, a well-charted path. There is argument over the degree to which it may be accelerated by good teaching, but some acceleration seems to be possible. The job of education is, in part, to encourage this acceleration by assisting children in the acquisition of knowledge and understanding. Education is about working with the developing child to build worthwhile knowledge. By knowledge we mean facts, certainly, but also skills and procedures, as well as a system of interrelated concepts. Of course, as we have said, there is room for argument about what that knowledge ought to be, and we shall return to that issue later. For the moment, it is sufficient to say that education is about working with development so as to enlarge children's understanding of the world. In this sense, it is goal-directed.

We know from studies of mothers with babies and young children and from our own work in both the voluntary and state sectors of provision for the under-fives, that adults hold expectations for the actions and understandings that even very young children ought to acquire and that they steer children towards those goals. We made these points in the previous chapter but repeat them here partly in response to some current notions that provision for the under-fives is predominantly one of care and requires minimal training, and partly in order to raise questions about the extent to which a curriculum for the over-fives should influence the curriculum to be experienced by younger children.

Child development studies have shown that adults in interaction with very young children start by inducting them into acceptable ways of operating in their social worlds. An example of this is the way a caregiver carries out what are termed 'proto-conversations' with the baby held in his or her arms. In these proto-conversations, the adult engages the child in the conversation and acts as if the child can join in the turn-taking of a real conversation. Experience of proto-conversations leads babies into the give and take of the one-to-one conversations that are central to effective communication in Western societies. An emphasis on social training predominates. But it is a social training which provides the skills necessary for undertaking later learning. Fontana and Edwards (1985) similarly found that nursery school teachers placed social control aspects of their work above the development of children's autonomy. These teachers justified this concern with turn-taking, give and take, and awareness of others as the first stage without which children could not begin to learn anything else.

Early years practitioners seem to set expectations and establish patterns of behaviour that make the management of groups of children possible and create behaviour patterns that ensure conformity beyond school settings. In this way, early years workers are preparing children for future demands. The sets of expectations with which early years specialists operate are social curricula. These curricula will include waiting one's turn at the slide, helping others, eating in ways that don't offend and keeping quiet while an adult is talking.

Physical curricula are also evident in all forms of provision for the under-fives. The development of small and large muscles, hand–eye coordination and balance feature large in the activities of young children. Here, even if an overt curriculum is not planned, it is driven by the resources available, what children can do when they use those resources, and the selections of resources made by adults.

Both social and physical development involve learning useful skills and concepts. These skills and concepts have not simply unfolded from the innate capacities of the child. Instead, they have been stimulated and shaped by the children's interactions with adults and other resources in the environment. These interactions are not random but are shaped by adults' views of appropriate responses. Vygotsky talks of the way in which adults mediate between the wider cultural expectations and the learner. It is this mediation process that we call teaching, and nowhere is it more difficult than in the very early years of educational provision. Note that this means that in so far as education for the under-fives has goals, it also has a curriculum. Often in practice that curriculum is neither explicit, planned long-term, nor coherent. This can lead to difficulties. These difficulties are evident in day-to-day planning, communicating purposes to parents and justifying the maintenance of provision to government.

The need for social and physical curricula in the education of the under-fives is often felt to be self-evident. A disruptive child or one without a sense of balance will have immediate difficulty in functioning and will need to learn how to overcome these gaps in performance. At first glance, it seems to be less necessary for children under five to follow a curriculum that is organized around a selection of important knowledge, which might indeed be structured around subjects such as English, art or mathematics. Yet quite clearly it happens. The academic curriculum of the under-fives can be seen, for example, in the repeated formats of counting rhymes, in the categorization processes of sorting and sequencing activities, and in the acquisition of a sense of audience in the telling of news.

Provision for the under-fives, when done well, as David *et al.* (1992) have advised, is purposeful and relevant to the children's future lives. In other words, it is planned within a broad framework and a selection of what is relevant. We would wish to argue that this planning needs to be made more explicit and open to discussion. As under-five practitioners become more used to discussing all aspects of their educational provision, it will become easier to resist the crass attacks made on this phase of provision.

Where children's curriculum acquisition becomes really problematic for those working with the under-fives is in the fleeting nature of much of the children's knowledge and understandings. Because the thinking of very young children is so extensively driven by cues in the context, it is often impossible to be sure what a child has learnt. One might think that a pattern of financial exchange had been understood only to find that a boy refuses to buy any of the dolls left in the 'toy shop' because he doesn't want girls' toys. At the same time, he may not be able to make it clear that this is the reason for his refusal to go through the motions and demonstrate or practise his grasp of exchange.

We would wish to argue that, while there is a very strong case to be made for keeping the assessment and accountability aspects of national curricula well away from the provision for the under-fives, less can be said for keeping a version of the curriculum itself at a distance. To paraphrase Bruner, there is nothing that cannot be taught to anyone provided it is taught in a way that can help them make sense of it. This does not mean that average four-year-olds should have to deal with the same tasks as average six-year-olds, but that the key concepts that justify the tasks of six-year-olds can also be incorporated into the activities available for a four-year-old. This now takes us on to what is a curriculum. Is it a set of tasks, a set of ideas or a set of skills? How is it derived? Why do we need one?

Elements of an early years curriculum

There are many views of curriculum. A serviceable definition is that it is the planned educational experiences made available to children. The notion of planning implies that curriculum is a purposeful attempt to work out certain educational goals. Those goals can be thought of as including attitudes and behaviour (the social curriculum), concepts, skills or ways of working, and information. We shall argue that conveying information to be remembered is not a large function of early years education.

However, curriculum cannot be constructed by simply identifying desirable concepts, ways of working and behaviours. The guru of progressive education, John Dewey, said that curriculum is a point on the continuum between the child and the subject. Through our discussion of the ideas of Vygotsky in Chapter 3, we have also placed the teacher on that continuum. The teacher mediates, designs and resources the curriculum for learners. We indicated in Chapter 3 that curricula are carried in the tasks that practitioners create for learners, and that the best designed tasks incorporate key concepts or ideas, and skills. This is further developed in Chapters 5 and 6. But other factors also influence curriculum. Bruner (1974) has advised us that we need to integrate knowledge about teaching, knowledge about learners and knowledge about knowledge itself if we want to avoid trivializing education – which he saw as a very real danger. Bruner (1974: 79–80) observed that:

> A generation ago the progressive movement urged that knowledge be related to the child's own experience and brought out of the realm of empty abstractions. A good idea was translated into banalities about the home, the friendly postman and dustman, then the community, and so on. It is a poor way to compete with the child's own dramas and mysteries.

Let us take Bruner's advice about the importance of each of these three dimensions, which need to be brought together for effective early years education, and take each in turn.

Knowledge about teachers: 'good practice' and the early years curriculum

Common sense tells us that it must be productive to identify key features of good practice and disseminate them, using them as a performance 'gold standard'. The national curriculum was based on this belief, with subject working parties being told to form curricula which embodied best – or at least good – practice in curriculum design. All schools were, then, to follow the agreed designs: excellence, so the government naively believed, was to be achieved through legislation, an Attila the Hun approach to achieving change.

One of us has argued that defining, identifying, documenting and disseminating good practice in both design and delivery is neither objective nor a matter of common sense (Knight and Smith 1989). Good practice, then, cannot be readily identified and labelled as a 'gold standard' to be met by all practitioners. Alexander (1992) took the same line in his discussion of good practice in primary education. Echoing the theme of his earlier work (Alexander 1984) that shibboleths and unquestioned ideologies have too much sway in primary schooling, he argued that 'good practice' is a deeply problematic concept. At the very least it embodies beliefs about the aims of education and about the best ways of discharging those beliefs. There is no way of resolving differences in values and the different beliefs and priorities associated with them, which is why education in open societies will always be a contentious and political matter. But surely research could identify those factors which are associated with the most effective pursuit of given educational aims and help us in the quest for the 'gold standard' of good practice?

Research into school and teacher effectiveness has flourished in recent decades. Whether it has provided answers to the questions we have in mind is disputable. Let us first dispose of a few methodological problems. If we want to know which teachers or schools are the most effective at, say, teaching reading, we need a pre-test of children's performance in reading followed by a period of reading learning in school, and then a post-test. What we will find is that children from certain socio-economic backgrounds will generally have the highest achievements, both on the pre-test and on the post-test. So great is the socio-economic influence that some researchers have said that schools hardly affect the life chances of children *in general*. Rather, it is home background which really counts. Clearly, we need a different measure of educational effectiveness. The preferred approaches measure children's progress – that is, the difference between their pre- and post-test scores. There are a number of technical complications here, but this method does offer a better, albeit far from perfect, view of the effect of the teacher or school. When allowances are made, statistically, for home background factors, it is seen that schools with children of similar achievements on entry produce children with quite different results on exit (Sammons *et al.* 1993). Schools – and teachers – it seems do make a difference.

There are three reasons why school effectiveness research of this kind will not resolve early years practitioners' difficulties in understanding curriculum. The first is that it is a leap from describing the conditions in which it appears that children do well to using those insights to improve practice. Knowing what is associated with effective education does not make it much easier to be effective. For example, it may be that an effective school is a happy school, but how does one make a rancorous school into a happy one? Second, there is the worrying phenomenon that effectiveness is unstable, even unpredictable. The school or the teacher which is effective this year may not be so next year. This must sap our confidence in findings based on *this* year's effective education practitioners (Sammons *et al.* 1993).

Third, from the perspective of early years education, the main problem is the pragmatic one of measuring children's achievements. Say we wish to know how effective Key Stage 2 practice is. We have year 2 assessments on file and year 6 assessments provide exit data. It is simple to calculate 'progress'. How, though, is progress to be measured in a nursery school or on entry to an infant department? Skilled practitioners are always noticing developments in the children with whom they work, but that is not a strong enough basis for identifying especially effective practices. We expect development in young children. Those who make judgements on the work of early years practitioners need measures sufficiently sensitive to tell us that *this* practice, teacher, school or assistant is especially effective and worth trying to emulate. They would like measures that prove to be fair and reliable when used in different schools. They want to be sure that they are detecting differences in educational effectiveness. The measures that they use have to be robust. As yet they do not exist.

The conclusion is that there is not even a pseudo-scientific method for identifying good practice in early years education, or its outcomes. The closest we get is for observers, such as the OFSTED inspectors, to judge schools against criteria which reflect someone's subjective notions of effective early years education. Unfortunately, the argument is circular, since the schools deemed to be effective are those which most closely approach the pre-set criteria of effectiveness. What is fatally absent is any measure of children's learning progress.

ofsted

So the early years curriculum cannot be informed by work on good practice alone. For the early years, the work on good practice is most useful at providing descriptions of the ways in which education workers try to achieve aims which are seen as desirable. Even then questions remain about how the less skilled practitioners learn from accounts of the work of the more skilled. These are questions which we cannot follow here. Instead, we turn to the idea that curriculum can be informed by the study of children.

Knowledge about learners: child development and the early years curriculum

We have already stated that studies of child development are essential to early years education. Four uses may be noted:

◀ They help us to map out the ways in which children are making sense of their experiences and the ways in which they are likely, in the future, to make sense of them. This is important for planning the next stages of learning, particularly if the aim is to bring children up against issues in their zones of proximal development (ZPDs).

◀ They alert us, in a systematic fashion, to things which children often find difficult or incomprehensible.

◀ They provide an account against which children's development may be set, allowing the identification of children who need special attention – whether by virtue of lack of progress or of rapid progress.

◀ In some cases, these studies contain suggestions for improving children's performance.

We have also stated that these studies have advantages over the knowledge which individuals build up through experience, since they represent systematic study of many different children and teachers in a variety of settings – that is, they are more catholic.

Curricula should, we believe, embody a view of child development. It has been a pity that the national curriculum has not often done so, with attainment target statements representing partly educated guesses. Psychologists have provided very little to help us to understand the relationships between the development of children's thinking skills and the acquisition of different types of knowledge.

Thankfully, there has been little support for the idea that the curriculum might comprise training children in typical Piagetian tasks used to assess development. Little value is seen in helping children to appreciate physical perspective by training them to describe models (of mountains, say) as though they were looking at them from a different angle; or in having them pour the same quantity of orange juice into different shaped containers so that they learn that the quantity of orange juice does not change, only its appearance.

One of the limitations of research into child development for early years practitioners is that it does not help us to decide on the content of the curriculum. If we take the line that many topics can be put into developmentally appropriate forms, we are faced with the awkward problem of which content to choose. Work on child development tells us much about how to teach and about the forms that children's understandings are likely to take. What it cannot do is tell us what children might learn about.

Another psychologically based approach to bringing children and the curriculum together has been to establish the children's needs and then to read a curriculum off from them. Needs analysis has been used to justify many practices (for example, the Schools History 13–16 Project was founded upon it), but Alexander (1992) has argued that it has been misapplied and has actually worked against children by denying them the broad curriculum to which we believe they are entitled. A major difficulty with it is that there are no agreed principles for identifying what children need (do they *need* religious education?), and identifying a need, such as physical security, simply shifts the problem of definition to the question 'what do we mean by physical security?'

Kellmer-Pringle (1980) identified four basic emotional needs:

◀ a need for love and security;
◀ a need for new experiences;
◀ a need for praise and recognition; and
◀ a need for responsibility.

What does this tell us about a curriculum for the early years? The main point is that, like the study of child development, it says nothing about the *content* of the curriculum. Its implications are mainly for the methods of learning and teaching that we might adopt. Now methods do, as we have said, constitute an important part of the curriculum, and it is likely that most early years workers would find no problem with the consequent ideas that the curriculum should:

◀ give children opportunities for success;
◀ give *all* children these opportunities, which means that teachers and the curriculum must be sensitive to differences of language, class, race, gender, development and ability;
◀ go beyond what children would experience if they were not in an educational programme – extend their horizons;
◀ provide plentiful opportunities for children to work independently (whether alone, in pairs or in larger groups), planning, playing, exploring, testing, making, creating and discovering: didactic learning has its place, but so do far more open-ended, albeit guided, forms of learning;
◀ be enjoyable and be associated with rewards (typically in the shape of esteem);
◀ be active both mentally and physically.

It is debatable whether this 'needs analysis' indicates in sufficient detail the scope of curriculum-as-process. Alexander (1992), for example, analysed curriculum-as-process under ten headings. Besides, curriculum-as-content remains an issue. Kellmer-Pringle's analysis of needs is strong as a *psychological* account, but schools are *cultural* institutions and education is a cultural artefact. What are children's cultural needs? Or, to put it differently, what are the important things children should learn about our society and world?

Knowledge about knowledge: cultural analysis and the early years curriculum

What procedures and concepts should children encounter? The notion of curriculum entitlement has become increasingly used to give an answer to this question. It is a social view of children's needs. The argument goes that a certain body of knowledge, understanding and skills is necessary for adults in our society. There is plenty of room for debate about what that body is, and the debate inevitably turns on the different values of participants. Yet, there is little argument that adults who lack numeracy, basic scientific concepts, literacy, healthy habits, some sense of the past and of other countries and cultures, an awareness of art, music and movement, are disadvantaged in important ways. It follows, then, that all children ought to be entitled to an education that inducts them into these forms of knowledge. The child who is deprived of an opportunity to learn something of scientific thinking is therefore being disadvantaged and treated unfairly. Now, the child may not enjoy doing science, but because science is a key part of our culture the child is entitled to a scientific education. In fact, because children are too young to recognize what they will need to be aware of in later life, they are to be compelled to do science. Besides, the country needs scientists. In this way, needs can be defined in terms of what the citizens of the future are expected to need, and in terms of what the government believes will be important to the country in the future. This last reason explains the prominence given to primary science since 1978 and the more recent inclusion of technology in the curriculum.

This approach to curriculum planning inevitably implies a broad curriculum. Of course, one would not knowingly include unteachable material in it, but since most areas of human experience can be represented by children in some worthwhile, albeit imperfect, way, that still implies a broad curriculum. So what might be the content of this broad curriculum to which early years children are entitled? Views differ somewhat, but not as much as might be imagined.

According to Chambers (1990), there are eight distinguishable varieties of experience for young children: knowledge of mathematics and logic; empiricist knowledge, such as 'the big ball hit the small ball and caused it to move; rain falling on soil makes mud' (p. 52); scientific knowledge; knowledge of persons and their minds; moral knowledge; experience and awareness of the arts and the aesthetic domain; religion; philosophy. Curtis (1986) identified seven skills and competencies: self-awareness; social; cultural; communication; perceptual and motor; analytical and problem working; creative/aesthetic. While her list is not particularly forthcoming about curriculum content, it is nonetheless plain that the curriculum should be a broad one.

A position paper by the National Association for the Education of Young Children (NAEYC) and the National Association of Early Childhood Specialists in State Departments of Education (NAECSSDE) also stipulates a broad curriculum (NAEYC/NAECSSDE 1991). Fourteen areas are described, including: 'understand and respect social and cultural diversity'; 'use language . . . become literate'; 'represent ideas and feelings through play, drama, dance and movement, music, art and construction'; 'construct understanding of . . . classifying, ordering, number, space and time'; 'acquire knowledge of and appreciation for the fine arts, humanities, and sciences'; and 'become competent in the management of their bodies and acquire basic physical skills . . . maintain a desirable level of health and fitness' (p. 28). Spodek and Saracho (1990) referred to the Chinese kindergarten curriculum which comprised music, language, maths, PE, art and general knowledge (that is to say, science and social studies).

A principled way of seeing this inclination towards a broad curriculum may be provided by the work of Gardner (1983). He began by rejecting, as had many before him, the notion of general intelligence. Instead, he said, we should see people as comprising multiple intelligences. His list is open to dispute, but the thrust of his ideas – that there is more to intelligence than verbal and logical skills – is interesting. He argued that there are linguistic, musical, logical-mathematical (including science), bodily–kinaesthetic (including art) and personal intelligences (inter- and intra-personal understandings). These intelligences are not just ways of thinking but also resemble forms of knowledge – subjects even – that are culturally accepted.

Whichever list is devised for planning, it is apparent that any attempt to develop cultural awareness implies a broad curriculum.

Cultural analysis suggests a broad curriculum and offers a way of identifying appropriate content. It follows that practitioners need to understand the basis of this broad curriculum. If they are to teach effectively, they also need to understand the central concepts, concerns and procedures of the principal components of this curriculum. We develop this point with reference to national curriculum subjects in Chapter 5. Without knowledge about knowledge – knowledge of the rationale behind the curriculum and of the discourses that it embodies – practitioners are poorly placed to work effectively as educators.

Elements of an early years curriculum: summary

Several conclusions may be drawn. First, there is a tradition of analysing the curriculum in terms of subjects which may be made accessible through tasks set for children. Second, that is not the only way of analysing it. Third, knowledge about teaching, development and about knowledge itself are also relevant. Fourth, some British reports have acknowledged that there are important matters, such as health education, environmental education and moral education, which ought to be covered and which might be overlooked if the curriculum were to be defined solely in subject terms. There is, then, something of a tension between a subject approach and an issues approach. Fifth, there is a case made that young children should encounter the same subjects as older children. That principle underlies the Chinese kindergarten curriculum. Sixth, we may have listed elements to be incorporated into the curriculum, but they do not prescribe the way in which the curriculum is to be created in the classroom. What all of these elements emphasize is the role of the teacher as mediator in Dewey's description of curriculum as a point lying between subjects and the child.

There is, however, a history of official indifference to curriculum content for the under-fives. Yet, if the principle holds good that there are content issues to be considered in early years education, then it is important that these earliest years are also considered. Early years workers do that, of course, but we suggest that more systematic consideration ought to be given to it, not least because the ways of understanding that become differentiated in these years are both many (children often display racial awareness and related attitudes then) and important.

Curriculum and making meaning

We are all too aware that once we accept a cultural analysis model of curricula and choose to discuss the given curriculum we are begging important questions of dominant culture. We do not accept that social inequality can be dealt with entirely within the more hidden social or interpersonal curriculum. Neither do we agree that value positions can be given, but rather that they need to be open to constant scrutiny. Having said that, we have a curriculum and to deny children access to what is currently considered to be a distillation of the knowledge and skills that they need is to disempower them. We also firmly believe that the scrutiny and questioning of given curricula can best be achieved by pupils once deep understanding is gained and once what is learnt is tested confidently against alternative value bases and social conditions.

We shall therefore examine the ways in which subject-specific meanings become widely understood and shared, and the role of educators in these processes. One premise for this discussion is our belief that if this process doesn't start early with all children, some will have a lot of catching up to do once they reach infant schooling. Later in this chapter, we shall explain why we have chosen to represent the content of early years curricula in terms of subjects, and in the next chapter we shall examine subjects in terms of their own integrity or coherence, uniqueness and compatibility with other subjects. We shall not dismiss out of hand the integration of subjects that occurs in topic work. We shall, however, offer some notes of practical caution. This caution is based largely on the need to acknowledge the complexities of the language we use to carry meanings when we talk as subject specialists. The subject-specific meaning in the language used by those who are inside the subject we shall call 'subject discourses'.

In order to clarify what we mean by a subject-specific meaning, let us return to our discussion of symbolic interactionism in Chapter 2. Mead's (1934) work enables us to see that in particular cultural groups we categorize our worlds in particular ways. In some families, for example, wealth, good looks and type of car are important categories in which people are placed and judged. In other families, the categories may be religious affiliation, educational attainment and musicality. Children in these families will categorize their life events in different ways from very early on. They will learn, in their interactions with adults and older children, what are the salient or important features and will mark or note them. They will either learn these features and use them, or will ignore them and as a consequence find it difficult to operate as a member of that family. Without sharing the meanings given to the categories, for example big car = good thing, they will be unable to engage in the family discourse in ways that make family sense.

If we move into the wider social world we can probably all recognize that gender, race and age are categories used when thinking about people. A questioning of these categories can imply a radical attack on received wisdom and the social fabric.

A comparison with subject knowledge at this point will take us into subject-specific meanings and discourses. There are ways of categorizing knowledge that are subject-specific. These categories we call concepts. We label these concepts and expect experts in each subject to more or less share common understandings of what we mean by those labels. These meanings and associated language labels are often subject-specific. State and media, which are concepts needed by scientists, do not mean the same things to historians, artists or English specialists. Equally, these are categories that help to hold a subject together and give it its logical coherence. There are other subject-specific elements, which we call procedures, ways of working or skills. Many skills, such as communication, analysis and hypothesizing, are shared by most subjects. Others, such as fair testing (experiment) and testing evidence for bias are particularly associated with specific subjects, in these cases, science and history. As learners we need access to both concepts and skills if we are to get inside the subject. Access comes with use of the subject language or discourse.

Subject expertise consists of mastery of the key categories or concepts and the patterns in which they relate one to the other. Children's expertise is of course a long-term aim. In the early years, we are talking about groundwork. This can most clearly be seen in the highlighting of key concepts and skills in the early years curriculum. This highlighting is most easily achieved through repeated use of the patterns and formats of the language or discourse of the subject.

Language and subjects

As we indicated in Chapter 3, in provision for the under-fives this highlighting is often carried out in a conversational mode. In these teaching and learning conversations, the child will take the lead in setting the pace and topic of conversation. The adult will use the conversation as the opportunity to mark or emphasize appropriate ways of seeing or interpreting what the child is discussing. Once a more clearly prescribed curriculum is encountered and the educational relay race is in train, teachers are under more pressure to direct the topics, but the highlighting, interpretative or mediation function of the practitioner remains similar. In both education for the under-fives and over-fives, the making of meaning is a joint enterprise in which the child is an active partner. We are saying that there is no reason why opportunities should not be provided for proto-conversations to take place on science, geography or mathematics.

The child is a partner but not a senior partner in these learning conversations. The adult is carefully mediating the curriculum using language and references which will allow the child to make sense. She or he may not always be using language that the child already knows, but will use language that is needed to enable the child to operate effectively inside the subject.

The 'do, talk and record' model of mathematical thinking developed by Floyd (1981) illustrates these points. The stages in this teaching and learning cycle start with children doing and talking alongside the teacher. This activity is followed by tasks in which children have the opportunity to do and talk in small groups and to begin to record and check. The final stage is recording in some publicly accessible way. The compatibility of this with the Vygotskian framework already offered is obvious. Its particular contribution is its emphasis on the use of mathematical language and the repetition of formats which consist of the terms needed for thinking mathematically. (You will recall our reference to the work of Wells on the relationship between language and thought in Chapter 3.)

The idea of discourse formats is a helpful one if we are to see how working within subjects is both useful and to be achieved. Bruner (1983), writing about how children begin to acquire language, describes how mothers lead their children into language formats so that they learn the rhythms, patterns and sounds of communicative speech, begin to anticipate them and learn to respond. The precise use of language formats also serves a purpose with slightly older children. Subjects have their own languages and their own discourse formats. The teacher in the mathematics interactions given in Chapter 3 was precise in her use of language. She did not interchange 'divide' and 'share', but stuck firmly to 'divide' in her discussion with the two six-year-olds.

We are all familiar with the large group activities in which children and practitioners appear to be in open-ended conversation but where actually the practitioner is carefully choosing language, asking children questions and expecting them to use the same language in their responses and is reshaping the responses if they don't quite do so. This is only possible where the practitioner has goals in the form of a curriculum. In those circumstances, it is also important for the practitioner to be clear about the ways in which the conversation can give rise to certain subject insights. This demands that practitioners have considerable curriculum knowledge.

Work in mathematics and science has particularly demonstrated the importance of precision in language and the acquisition of subject-specific language. These studies are of particular relevance to the early years curriculum where the domestication of learning tasks and the familiarity of language have frequently been key features of provision, with the result that subject-specific knowledge has not been an overt priority.

Walden and Walkerdine (1982, 1985) and Walkerdine (1988) undertook close examination of the mathematical experiences of children and the language in use in activities that had mathematical potential. Their work raised important questions about the effectiveness of domesticating these experiences. They argued that initially the domestication of mathematics in, for example, the home corner disadvantaged the boys, who were not as confident as the girls in this domestic setting. Later, the girls had to make a considerable leap from their comfortable, home-based mathematical concepts into more abstract conceptualizations. This leap is where the teacher has the very important function of offering a scaffolding to help in the transition from a limited contextual understanding to the more abstract conceptualization necessary for functioning in other situations. Walker and Walkerdine cautiously suggest that the problem girls have in handling abstract mathematical concepts may in some way account for the relative unpopularity of mathematics for some girls in the secondary phase.

Walkerdine was particularly concerned with language use and although her use of the term discourse is wider than ours, she makes some interesting points which give food for thought to early years practitioners. Her analysis of child and adult talk at the very least leads practitioners to question the lack of precision which goes hand in hand with what appears to be child-friendly language. As we have already noted, the teacher in the division conversation discussed in Chapter 3 was careful to use divide rather than share when she prompted the thinking of the two six-year-olds with whom she was working. Share is a word that has meanings which extend beyond the mathematical processes of division. A child may be told to share the playground bicycle, her bag of sweets, the box of crayons. Sharing for egocentric young children often means parting with something they would like to keep entirely to themselves.

Similarly, the words 'more' and 'less' have domestic or personal connotations: 'She has more than me', 'No you can't have any more', 'No more now, off to bed'. Little and big can also be quite fuzzy concepts: 'No you are too little to stay up' and 'You are a big boy so put your coat away' can be said to the same child in one conversation. Friezes which show big and small animals can confuse if, for example, the 'small rabbit' is actually represented as larger than the class pet rabbit. Clearly, children do cope with these possible confusions. They come to recognize the discourse in which they are operating. They differentiate between play in the home corner and the language allowed there, and mathematical tasks in the maths area and the language there. They learn to situate themselves inside a discourse, read the cues and operate with the expectations of that discourse. So they learn eventually that 'share' in mathematics does not have the connotations of injustice that it might have in the playground.

Most children eventually become adept at recognizing the cues and expectations of different discourses. What the work of Walkerdine and others suggests is that it may not be entirely necessary to extensively domesticate the language of mathematics in the early years. If children can recognize and operate within the specific discourses, why not give them early access to the language they will need in order to do so most effectively? Taking domestic language into mathematical discourse in the expectation that it will help children understand may be misplaced assistance. The words will mean something different in the precise language of mathematics. Young learners consequently have to discard previously held meanings and add new mathematical meanings to familiar words. It may well be easier to learn mathematical language in the first instance. The division discussion already mentioned showed that 'divide' presented no problems to the two young children involved.

We are arguing, then, that effective early years education involves teachers in managing a subtle interplay between knowledge about subjects and knowledge about the developing learner so that confusions are lessened and access to subject discourses is made easier.

In a study with junior school children, researchers from the Assessment of Performance Unit (APU) found a distinct difference in performance levels between two groups of children. The first group was given a simple experiment couched in domestic terms and the second group was presented with it as a scientific experiment. The second group outperformed those who were given the more domestic version (Froufe 1990). They appeared to be taking the experiment more seriously and used the language demanded by the scientific discourse within which they could clearly see themselves and the activity to be situated.

We know how much young children love playing with language and relish using the long words they acquire. Most young children know far more types of dinosaur than do most adults! If they acquire the dinosaur discourse, why not the mathematical one? We are therefore arguing that, provided the processes of discourse acquisition are paced and appropriately related to children's actions, quite complex subject-specific language can be introduced as frequently repeated elements or formats of the powerful and publicly understood discourses of specific subjects.

Subjects and integration

We have described the 'academic' curriculum in terms of subjects, which will seem an uncomfortable prospect to many early years practitioners. At best, subjects are something wished on schools through the national curriculum. At worst, they are constraining, arid abstractions insensitively wished on infant schools by clueless bureaucrats. We are aware of the antipathy that is felt towards subjects. In a recent paper, for example, Hurst (1993: 2) notes how the pressures on Key Stage 2 'exert downward pressure on teachers of younger children at Key Stage 1, and in nursery schools and classes. This forces teachers of young children to introduce a traditional curriculum based on "subjects" too soon'. Nevertheless, we say that subjects are not incompatible with early years education and that there are advantages to using subjects to think about the curriculum. It is not the subjects that are the problem. As Hurst (1993) hints, it is 'traditional' subject teaching that is the problem. The task of practitioners is to use subjects as a set of frameworks that help both practitioners and learners to identify and use the discourses and understandings that they contain.

At some point, beginning practitioners will need to arrive at understandings of the structure of the material of the early years curriculum. We suggest that this is best done through analyses of the nature of subjects. For one thing, this is well established in the branch of philosophy known as epistemology. Subjects are an accepted way of describing the knowledge that is important within our culture. This connects with our view that education is about adding the beginnings of culturally important understanding to child development. This is not, we believe, a way of imposing one set of values on children. A subject such as history or geography allows for many interpretations and for many values to be expressed. Subject thinking offers a way of organizing our knowledge. It does not compel us to accept any particular values. On the other hand, there is a case for saying that subjects describe many facets of our culture and that children are entitled to an education that sketches the main features of that culture.

Second, there is a long history of applying those analyses to education. Indeed, there is a growing body of research showing how important it is for teachers to understand the nature of subjects if they are to teach well (Bennett and Carré 1993; McNamara 1994). Third, we tend to draw upon subject insights when confronted with what we perceive to be problems. They are resources for problem solving and scaffolding for thinking. Subjects, then, are a convenient way in which to address questions about the purposes of learning, especially when subjects are understood and taught with an eye to encouraging learners to think about their applications and uses.

We agree that subjects can be presented in arid and abstract ways. It is also true that adult subjects are way beyond young children. Yet subjects can be translated into appropriately accessible forms and used to organize the curriculum that shapes the opportunities which teachers create and the discourses that they manage. Where subjects lead to shackled teaching and dullness, we would argue that the fault lies in the educational thinking and actions of practitioners more than in the subjects themselves. Given that teachers have not had the opportunity to be trained in developmentally appropriate ways of working with subjects, that is a plausible line.

A pervasive fear, though, is that a subject-based curriculum must be a fragmented curriculum. This would be unfortunate, given that it appears that young children do not make the many distinctions that adults do and tend to see things in more connected and holistic ways. But, as we have argued earlier, we should not underestimate the ability of children to read the cues of specific discourses and operate within them (you've only to listen to them playing families or schools). Consequently, there seems to be no reason why teachers should not themselves use subject insights and discourses as they plan integrated topics. One of us has argued that, even with the more prescriptive Key Stage 2 curriculum with all its attendant knowledge demands, it is eminently possible to continue several forms of topic work (Knight 1993). In Key Stage 1, we can see that both the content of the science, geography and history curricula, and their ways of working, can be rolled together without violence to any of the three subjects. The content would be the local environment addressed from the three subject perspectives, while procedures which the three subjects share include planning, investigating, recording, interpreting and communicating.

It is, we claim, a myth that subjects have no value for early years curriculum planning, and we notice that an authoritative American paper on the curriculum for three- to eight-year-olds outlines a curriculum based on a wide range of subjects (NAEYC/NAECSSDE 1991). It is a myth that planning with subjects in mind will damage early years education, for we strongly believe that young children can cope with a variety of discourses. It is a myth that this approach would mark the end of topic work and integrated approaches to the curriculum. Rather, we claim that subjects offer powerful and useful ways of organizing education. However, as the government has recognized, there are themes and issues that lie outside subjects and which ought also to have a place in the curriculum, as we have acknowledged in our discussions of the social curriculum.

The power of the discourse

Early years practice has been informed by a range of ideas or theories. To return to the discussion at the beginning of this chapter, we note that sometimes these ideas appear to compete with each other, as when a belief that learning is enhanced by allowing the child's innate capacities to reveal themselves is countered by a belief that children need to be prepared for the social conditions in which they will have to operate. We hope that our discussions so far suggest that our response to the two beliefs just outlined is 'well, it is a bit of both'. Theories of learning emerge from the observations of learners, they raise new questions which can only be tackled by more observation and so theories are modified, elements are discarded and new aspects are highlighted and taken into practice. An example of the development of theory and its current relevance to practice can be seen in the impact of Piaget's work.

Piaget, because he was interested in how knowledge developed in young minds, saw development in terms of progress towards abstract thought and the formal manipulation of knowledge. Context was not a priority in his concern to describe the development and organization of *general* knowledge structures in children's minds. Donaldson (1978) was a key text because it looked at Piaget's work from an educational perspective and allowed us to see the extent to which context impacted on the way that children interpreted situations and reacted to them. She talked of the importance of human sense and how children contextualized problems and could solve them in ways that could be seen to take into account contextual cues. The challenge then facing educators was to move children away from a reliance on context, so evident in young children, to an ability to disembed or decontextualize their reasoning. Although the demands of this kind of work are a feature of the work of some teachers of older children, they warrant some discussion in this text as they relate to the groundwork to be done by early years specialists.

The now classic study of child street traders in Brazil (Carraher *et al.* 1990) illustrates very clearly the limitations on thinking and performing mathematically that result from an inability to use the powerful publicly understood discourse of mathematics. The children worked as street traders for their families, selling fruit. They had an average age of 11.2 years. They performed quite complex mathematical transactions while trading but did not use the formal rules of mathematics. The personal rules they did use worked well for the tasks they met on the street but were heavily context-dependent. In classrooms, the children were unsuccessful in tasks which were comparable but presented out of context. The following example from the work of Carraher and colleagues demonstrates this:

Male (12 years old)
Informal test
Customer: I'm going to take four coconuts. How much is that?
Child: Three will be 105 plus 30, that is 135 . . . one coconut is 35 . . . that is . . . 140!

Formal test
Child resolves the item 35×4 explaining out loud 4 times 5 is 20, carry the 2; 2 plus 3 is 5, times 4 is 20. Answer written: 200.

This is a splendid example of the way that learning in a particular context may be proficient while similar proficiency may not be shown in different contexts. This is important because education involves fostering understandings that are general enough to be applied successfully to new problems and situations. Sometimes this point is overlooked by people who are so anxious that learning takes place in comfortable contexts. We would not deny the importance of that. We would want to say that the educator's job is to help children to generalize that learning to novel situations. In this sense, learning always implies eventually moving from the comfortable and familiar to unfamiliar settings. It implies the slow formation of abstract knowledge.

The following example from the work of a ten-year-old Lancashire pupil indicates the importance of establishing the groundwork of rules that are universally applicable if the learner is to operate powerfully within the discourse at later stages of life. James was working on a computer programme which was designed to test and increase his speed on subtraction calculations. Despite the programme's thirty-second speed limit he began the first calculation by using his fingers. What follows is the conversation with his teacher.

Teacher: How did you work that out?
James: Don't know Miss.
Teacher: Tell me how you did these sums?
James: Sixty-one take away five is sixty-six.
            Forty-three take away five. I take five away from three,
            that leaves two. I take that from forty. Get forty-eight.
Teacher: What did you do wrong?
James: [Pause] . . . I added it.
Teacher: Try taking away.
James: Twenty-one take away four. Four take away one leaves
            three. Take that away from twenty leaves seventeen.
            Eighty-one take away five. Five take away one gets four.
            Take that away from eighty – leaves seventy-six.

James continued in this way with the remaining sums.

Let us return to our theories of the development of theory. Others have worked with the ideas presented by Donaldson and have taken them further to issue the challenge that perhaps the real issue is not the ability to decontextualize but to recontextualize. That is, for the learner to be able effectively to read the cues available in a particular subject discourse and to be able to operate within that discourse in a variety of settings. So the effective learner in mathematics can take skills acquired in one mathematical context, read the demands of a new mathematical context and apply the same skills in ways that meet those new demands. The works of Walkerdine (1988) and Solomon (1989) have helped us to see how children enter a set of mathematical practices through learning how to operate in those practices.

Their work does have important implications for those who are establishing the groundwork of learning. In order to operate successfully in the later stages of education, children will eventually have to be able to identify the knowledge and skills they possess and the demands of the contexts in which they will operate and, above all, have the confidence to apply this knowledge and skills to new tasks. Mastery of a discourse involves the acquisition of the key concepts associated with that discourse and the confident use of the skills without which they could not have acquired the conceptual map of the subject or element of the subject. Mastery is evident in the ability to use these understandings in skilful ways in unfamiliar settings. Mastery of a discourse consequently empowers the learner to operate with the new demands. Subject discourses give access to subject knowledge and empower learners in their operations within the subject.

Conclusion

Young children are entitled to a curriculum. We have suggested that subjects offer a valuable resource for planning that curriculum. Among other things, they represent key aspects of our culture and they bring with them their own discourses. In discussing the elements of an early years curriculum, we have made it clear that we do not favour making the early years into feeble copies of Key Stage 2, and we believe that there is no reason why integrated approaches should be displaced.

In a nutshell, our position is that when thinking about effective early years education, we must ask the question: 'Effective at what?' We have argued that subjects provide the 'what', bearing in mind that the curriculum is greater than just a collection of subjects. We therefore turn, in the next chapter, to discussions of the central features of the subjects that are likely to feature in an early years curriculum.

Points for reflection

1 In the light of this discussion, what do you think an early years practitioner needs to know? What are the implications for INSET?
2 What arguments are there against our position? Do you think that they have more force than ours? If so, what conclusions do they lead to in respect of:

◄ the nature of the curriculum;
◄ curriculum planning;
◄ educational practice in the early years;
◄ practitioner education?

Further reading

The work of Jerome Bruner (1983) is based on reflection upon considerable work with young children. More recent work by Alexander (1992) questions a number of assumptions about good practice and children's needs. His book is not focused upon the early years, though. David McNamara's (1994) discussion of the primary school curriculum raises similar questions to ours about the need to value subject knowledge as an element of professional practice.

SUBJECTS AND
THE EARLY YEARS
CURRICULUM

We have argued that subjects are a resource to be used in constructing the early years curriculum. In this chapter, we will do two things. The first is to look at each of the nine national curriculum subjects and religious education, explaining what we see as special about each of them. In this sense, the chapter is a practitioner's guide to the essence of these subjects. The second is to set these reviews in the context of five themes relevant to the idea of a subject-led curriculum:

◀ The importance of identifying the key concepts of a subject. We shall use science and religious education to illustrate this.
◀ The place of discovery learning in a subject-led curriculum, with reference to maths and geography.
◀ The meaning of knowledge, taking history as an example.
◀ Progression and the re-presentation of material, with technology and music providing the examples.
◀ Topic work and subject integration, with reference to English, physical education and art, and discussion of cross-curricular themes.

These twin aims mean that we shall use each subject to illustrate a more general theme. Of course, we could have chosen different mixes of subjects and themes, using geography, for example, to illustrate the issue of integration, physical education to illustrate re-presentation, art to illustrate discovery, maths to illustrate knowledge, and history to illustrate key concepts. We shall also have things to say about each subject that are not linked to the theme which it is illustrating, aiming to convey something of its flavour.

Science and concept development

As the national curriculum was being formed, it was increasingly said that children ought to learn certain scientific content and principles – science was to be seen as content as well as process knowledge. This marked a break with earlier trends which emphasized the importance of children *doing* science. What science they did was not a matter of much concern.

If children are to work on certain scientific themes, then an aim is to develop the appropriate concepts. However, a considerable body of research (Anderson and Smith 1987) shows how children's scientific knowledge is deeply misconceived. Wrong ideas abound, for example that plants are not living things, that gravity acts more forcibly on massive objects than on lesser ones. The development of these well-documented and pervasive alternative concepts has been mapped in science. We must say here that alternative concepts also exist in other subjects too. In science they have been especially carefully studied.

Taking this research, we can see children's concept development as a path from a very wrong concept, to a less wrong concept, to an even less wrong concept. Education is about moving children from a spontaneous concept – one based on intuitive understanding of the world – to a better concept. An example would be where children develop their spontaneous concept that heavy things sink into the more formal concept that the shape of the object affects whether it sinks or not. At a much later stage, they will then meet the much more adequate concept of specific density. Yet, physics undergraduates and primary teachers are both likely to hold false concepts, and answer wrongly questions such as 'What forces are at work on a coin that has been tossed?' or 'In what direction do forces operate on a goldfish that is stationary in water?' These particular alternative concepts are not important for early years teaching, but they neatly illustrate the proposition that conceptual learning is a path from wrong to less wrong: few people make it to the 'right' concept. An important implication of this research is that while it would be nice if children did learn the 'right' answer, it would be foolish to exaggerate the importance of this in the early years. Alternative concepts are highly resilient to teaching, and disappointment goes hand in hand with our attempts to change them.

Change can be made, though. We need to bear in mind that these are unlikely to be changes from a poor concept to a perfect one. Despite teaching, children are likely to hold onto faulty notions. Achieving that improvement involves a constructivist approach to science.

Constructivism is derived from psychological work, such as Piaget's and Vygotsky's. Learners make sense of the world by forming concepts to describe their experiences. These concepts are interrelated in the brain and both concepts and their organization survive until dissonance arises. Dissonance occurs when the mind gives up its normal habit of perceiving things that fit the existing concepts (what Piaget called assimilation) and notices something that doesn't fit. At this point, the normal reaction is to do nothing, or perhaps to mutter 'how interesting'. Sometimes, dissonance is created. Concepts and structures *may* be modified to incorporate this new information (accommodation, in Piaget's terms). Following this model, we can say that science teaching is about creating dissonance (not easy, given the forces of assimilation) and prompting an accommodation that is better than the previous concept. So, the tasks of the practitioner are:

◀ to have an idea of which concepts are to be improved;
◀ to know which alternative concepts children are likely to hold;
◀ to provide situations in which children may be encouraged to notice discrepancies;
◀ to use that observation to get children to suggest an explanation;
◀ to get them to play with the explanation, making fair tests of it;
◀ to get them to apply and consolidate their conclusions.

Following our line in earlier chapters, we must add that this will often be done with familiar materials and, in the first instance at least, in familiar situations. Baking, washing, sand and water play, all offer opportunities for this approach to concept development.

Feasey (1993) suggests that Science Attainment Target 1, which relates to scientific processes of enquiry, should be pursued through five steps, which we see as consistent with a constructivist approach to science:

1 Examining the similarities (for example, between objects that sink, or stick together, and those that don't).
2 Choosing appropriate equipment for that observation (lenses or balances, for example).
3 Focusing on key points (weight, shape, size, slipperiness).
4 Using a range of senses in doing it.
5 Using scientific knowledge to make use of the observations (concluding that shiny things stick together and testing it; suggesting that things that stick together are magnetic, and testing that).

This is a demanding set of requirements. It stands in contrast to a common assumption that is often made that science may be taught to children without them realizing it. Indeed it may. That does not mean, however, that the teacher can simply expose children to situations that may prompt scientific thinking, which is a position often associated with the 'unaware science' stance. We have consistently argued the opposite. In a book that may be recommended as a source of ideas for teaching science in the early years, Browne (1991: 20) said that 'it is highly questionable whether it is feasible to expect children to "discover" generally accepted scientific facts virtually unaided'. Elsewhere, she criticized an 'overestima-tion of what it is possible for children to discover through observation' (p. 11), albeit with reference to Victorian object lessons. Her position is not that children should therefore be taught science in a purposeful and ex-plicit manner: the contributors to her book have plenty to say about ways in which play activities may be used for these purposes. The point is that the teacher needs to provide scaffolding to help children see what they are seeing. In other words, time needs to be made for discussion and reflection. Treating science as something children can do without being aware of it is not wrong in principle, but it is certainly sterile if that means that science work is about physical activity without thought and conceptual growth. Both depend upon the practitioner intervention, sometimes by drawing attention to what children have done, sometimes by asking for ideas, sometimes by asking if there are alternatives that might have advantages, and sometimes by getting children to compare and evaluate what they are doing. This, of course, is no more than what we have said in earlier chapters, but we stress it here because as late as 1989 HMI found that two-thirds of infant science was inadequate.

With preschool children there are many possibilities for exploring the characteristics of materials and plants through direct, hands-on play. The problem for practitioners is how ambitious they should be in trying to draw out conceptual awareness from these activities. The same is true for most of the foundation subjects too.

Science is not only about improving children's concepts. It is also a method of enquiry. The idea of experimentation, or of a fair test, is central to science work. The national curriculum recognizes that with its Science Attainment Target 1. Unfortunately, it is often, claimed Browne (1991: 16), 'an exercise in memory rather than an opportunity to explore the natural world'. Yet, as Harlen (1993: 40), an expert on primary science, said: '*the development of understanding in science is thus dependent on the ability to carry out process skills in a scientific manner*' (original emphasis).

In the 1980s, science was often seen as teaching children such a way of working. It was entirely compatible with beliefs about good early years practice, so that investigations of 'floating and sinking' could be playful, hands-on investigations, well within children's scope. There was a feeling that this practical work was often over-directed by teachers (HMI 1991), which is probably a normal response to a situation where practitioners feel under pressure to 'produce the goods'. We shall meet this dilemma again. On the one hand, there is a belief that discovery learning is vital in the early years, but on the other, there is the view that more directive teaching is needed where it is important that children master something. This is a dilemma that will pervade *all* of the curriculum, since the curriculum is important in its entirety, even traditionally marginalized subjects such as art, music and physical education.

In recent years, teachers have felt even more pressured, raising the spectre of over-formal science teaching in the early years. We need to insist that effective learning depends on children developing concepts through the activity of 'hands-on' science. If children do not develop the notion of controlling variables, in the guise of a fair test, then they are not learning science.

In this respect, science closely resembles the foundation subjects. Its methods are not dissimilar to those used in technology, art, geography and, perhaps, history. The concept of experiment or fair testing is often presented as fundamental to scientific enquiry, which it is, and as distinctive of science, which it isn't. Science shares other ways of working with other subjects, placing emphasis on observing, asking questions, devising and modifying fair tests, suggesting conclusions, communicating and then discussing those communications. Thus with science we see an interplay between the concepts and the procedures. We also see that those procedures provide one way of integrating scientific enquiry with other subjects.

Religious education and concept development

Religious education (RE) is an exceptionally complex subject and teaching it to young children is equally complex. We see two elements to RE. One is the spiritual side, concerned with the idea of a spirit that survives death. This side can be tackled in two ways – by developing general spiritual concepts (about a creator, myth, symbols, magic and miracles, the soul) and by increasing children's knowledge of specific religions and their rites. The second side is moral education (ME). While ME does not have to be put in a religious setting, all religions contain strong moral views, so RE and ME are invariably linked.

The simplest aspect of RE is that concerning children's knowledge of religions. In English maintained schools, the Schools Curriculum and Assessment Authority has suggested that 50 per cent of RE should be Christian in character, although two other religions may also be dealt with by the time children reach the age of seven. Although it may not be the most relevant of things to many children, information about key faiths can be conveyed through stories and through the celebration of various festivals. Another line is to look at what it means to be a Hindu, Muslim, Buddhist or Christian, which might be done through activities on the lives of people of different faiths, much as history and geography look at peoples of different times and places.

Yet if we wish to shape general, religious concepts, we need to get behind the stories and deal with wider religious concepts. An obvious problem is that religious concepts differ from science concepts. They cannot be tested and proven. We suggest that an important goal is to try and shape some meanings around words like 'church', 'religion', 'mosque', 'belief', 'Allah' and 'God'. The goal of this type of concept development is to shape a general understanding that many people believe that when they die something lives on: that there are different accounts of what this is; that we call different accounts different religions; that different religions worship different gods; that different gods expect to be worshipped in different ways; and that different religions go with different lifestyles.

An obvious difficulty is that it is hard to map out the way in which such concepts develop. There is no simple equivalent to the descriptions of concept development that exist for science. This is not true for other subjects, although we have the best developmental maps for maths and science and little research has been done into art concepts. Yet in one sense concept development in RE can be simpler than in science, where children's commonsense explanations get in the way of a scientific view of the world. In another sense it is harder, since we are dealing with the most abstract aspects of human existence. What is clear is that there is little point in providing children with information about different religions unless work is done on these fundamental concepts. Without it, information on religions gets reduced to the status of curious fairy tales.

With moral education we are on surer ground, since issues of faith do not come into play to such an extent. In the early years, we are interested in forming knowledge of right and wrong, and as we noted in Chapter 2, much social learning is to do with mastering such norms. There is also conceptual development to consider alongside this work on rules of behaviour. Young children often judge actions by their consequences alone. So throwing stones is bad but throwing stones and accidentally breaking a window is worse. The child's reasoning is that it is the consequence that defines the morality of the action. A more sophisticated concept is that we ought to judge according to the intention behind the actions. In some ways, like science concepts, this is counterintuitive. To children it seems wrong to treat the same the person who broke a window and the one who was just throwing stones. However, the moral principle of judging an action by its intent is a fundamental one in our society. It is intention that separates murder from manslaughter. So this is, therefore, a good concept for us to lead children towards.

Likewise, people interested in moral education speak of the golden rule. This means treating others in the ways in which one would like to be treated oneself. There are plenty of possibilities for embedding this precept in the social curriculum as well as using it in talk about religious stories. We mention it partly because it is a key notion in moral education, but also to show that developing children's concepts, in this case a concept of fairness, need not make difficult demands on practitioners. What it does demand is that the teacher, being aware of the subject, is also aware of the need to think about good early years practice in order to identify the types of context in which key concepts may be developed. It is a matter of using subjects to guide the ways in which the learning environment is shaped (Chapter 6) and the focus of the tasks that we set (Chapter 3).

Mathematics and learning through discovery

What do we mean by 'mathematics'? Although the Cockcroft Report on mathematics (1982) saw it as a form of communication and a source of interest, there are regular calls for more attention to be paid to 'the basics'. Who could disagree? The snag is that what is often meant by 'the basics' is nothing of the sort. It usually means attention to formal number work and the four rules of arithmetic, which is just a part of mathematics work, as both the Cockcroft Report and the national curriculum make clear. However, schools and nurseries still face pressure for formal teaching of number, with unfortunate results. First, mathematics tends to deal in right and wrong answers. Formal teaching of mathematics can give a lot of children plenty of experience of wrong answers – of failure. This can lead, even at early ages, to 'maths phobia', which Cockcroft identified as a major obstacle to more effective mathematics teaching. A second problem with formal mathematics is that often children do not understand the abstract concepts that we use to describe reality, let alone the routines for manipulating those mathematical concepts. They have not built up a mathematical understanding through play, experience, problem working and practical application. There has been too little discovery in their learning, which is, in fact, shallow. Desforges and Cockburn (1987) published a small-scale study showing how teachers strove desperately to cope with infant maths, doing so by teaching procedures at the expense of developing understanding. What children needed was more practical, hands-on mathematics. What they got was more practice in routines that they didn't understand.

We are decidedly not against formal mathematics. As Cockcroft noted, some things have to be learned by heart. We criticize (a) pushing formal mathematics too early and (b) emphasizing formal mathematics at the expense of experiences on which understanding may be based. Published mathematics schemes, however good, lend themselves to formal mathematics, done individually, at the expense of group work and talk, which Cockcroft also valued. We are, then, making two claims. One is that it would be as foolish to stop three-year-olds learning to count as it would be to stifle older children's interest in historical dates. Yet preschool mathematics is about shaping *understandings* of number, shape and space. Formal manipulation of number is not a priority, although it may well be a product. Second, mathematics in years 1 and 2 needs to be more like preschool maths in approach: preschool maths should not become more like year 2 maths.

The national curriculum for maths includes the key elements identified by Cockcroft. Shuard (1986), a member of the committee, has identified those elements as: investigation; problem-solving; the practise of skills; exposition by the teacher; children discussing and explaining their work; and practical work. We could rephrase this to say that there is a place for discovery, for teacher-led work, for teacher-structured work and for practice. In the past, discovery learning was criticized because it was supposed that children were left to discover propositions that were beyond them and that they were left without the help needed to gain and understand general propositions and procedures. That criticism is a fair one. Discovery needs to be seen, as we showed in Chapter 2, as a part of a learning cycle. Good teaching includes arranging things so that discoveries are likely to be fruitful and so that they are rounded off with the teacher's support. Under these circumstances, even a subject such as mathematics, which so often trades in right and wrong answers, is suited to discovery methods.

Take problem solving, where we are asking children to discover a mathematical solution to a problem in their environment. An example would be asking them what is the best way of measuring the classroom, leading them towards an understanding of the importance of standard measures. Or they might be asked 'what is the lightest?'; or to measure the performance of a working model; or to weigh ingredients; or to present data from their fair tests, perhaps in graphical form; or to make nets as a way of making three-dimensional shapes. The strategies that they might use could follow these hints (Charles and Lester 1984, quoted in Shuard 1986):

> *General strategies*:
> Look for patterns – generalize
> Use deduction or induction
> Work backwards
> Guess – and then check
> Solve a similar problem first
>
> *Helping strategies*:
> Re-read the problem (for older children only!)
> Look for key words or phrases (ditto)
> Write down important information (ditto)
> Make an organized list, chart or drawing
> Experiment, or act out the problem
> Try the problem with easier numbers

To this list should be added discussion, when different groups compare their conclusions and when the practitioner tries to direct learners' attention to salient features, and away from any irrelevant ones, such as attractiveness or colour, that may be proffered.

Implicit in this account is the idea that children will work as groups on problem working, extending the range of possibilities that is offered as ways of resolving the problem and encouraging discussion in the process. This is consistent with the position taken by Vygotsky, which we discussed in Chapter 3. Where small groups (say of three children) of differing abilities are concerned, the more able benefit from having to explain their thinking and the less able benefit from the 'teaching' of the more able. As with all groups, though, rules are needed to inhibit one individual from dominating. There is also a case for keeping the more assertive children separate from the less confident. However, although group organization is common in maths, as in other subjects, research has tended to find that children do not work *as* groups. Effective practitioners are aware of this pitfall in group organization and monitor classroom activity for signs that children need to be helped to work *as* groups.

One point needs particular attention. Children bring alternative concepts to their science work. In mathematics, they develop 'buggy routines', methods that work sometimes but not always. 'Buggy routines' are highly resistant to formal teaching. Researchers have studied hundreds of them. Although discovery learning is one source of these 'buggy routines', there is evidence that they also come from formal mathematics teaching. It is believed that well-structured practical mathematics work can help to stop them developing, since it helps children to understand why the methods that they use are the right ones. In that setting, then, practitioners do need to complement discovery and practical work, as we have said, with presentation of the formal, correct procedures.

A related problem is that children often fail to see the link between discovery and practical work and the formalized methods used on paper. The result is that a child who is learning partly through discovery 'is little better off than the child who is taught the formalized method only by demonstration' (Shuard 1986: 84). 'It seems', Shuard adds, 'that the intermediate step of making the link between concrete embodiment and formalization is often missing in a child's experience'. The solution is not more practical work, nor more formal teaching, since that lacks the necessary basis in practical work. What is needed is direct, purposeful intervention by practitioners to help children to see that the formal proposition is another way of describing what they have learnt through practice. Hughes (1986) has shown how some children do not see the value of using conventional symbols such as +, − and ×. Four- and five-year-olds can fail to connect practical work that has shown them that three dots (∴) is the same as 3. Teaching and curriculum planning must undertake the task of helping children to transfer the knowledge that they have gained in a practical setting to the general context of formal mathematics. It is a formidable task, but if 'the basics' means anything for early years mathematics, this is it. Nothing is more basic than understanding, and understanding depends on practical work to discover possibilities and to practise the application of procedures.

One reason that Hughes gives for children's difficulties with formal mathematics is that they fail to see the point of it: '*When children first encounter written arithmetic in school, it serves no obvious purpose*' (Hughes 1986: 170, original emphasis). This points to a breakdown in the learning cycle in that practitioners have failed to embed the connections between the practical, exploratory work and the generalized and decontexted formulae and procedures that describe it. It also shows the perils of exposing children to the discourse of a subject unless great care has been taken to connect it with children's embedded experience and understandings. The position we reach is that subject learning in the early years is a double dialogue: a dialogue between practical and formal, and between contexted understandings and the generalized public discourse of subjects.

It is hard to see how, if mathematics were not planned from a subject perspective, it would be possible to have a fit curriculum for mathematics, combining practical opportunities, talk and exposition in order to develop awareness, and more importantly, confident understanding. Nor can they be achieved through the excess of formal mathematics teaching that is seen in many classrooms.

Geography and learning through discovery

Let us begin with the question of whether geography is a fit subject for young children. Much received wisdom says that it is not. An uncomplicated definition of geography is that it is work to do with the lives of people in different places. The problem is that the received wisdom about early childhood says that young children need to work with concrete materials, through experience, using play as they follow their interests in material that makes 'human sense'. 'Children', say David *et al.* (1992: 5), 'do not learn as successfully if they are simply told or shown what to do rather than given the opportunity to experiment for themselves'. We have argued that mathematics can and should provide space for discovery learning. But geography can be seen to be about adults and adult experience, hence removed from children's daily experience and concerns. This is particularly true where the adults are within cultures that do things differently from the life to which children are accustomed. Children's common reaction is to label these differences as daft and to diminish these different peoples. Knight (1987) has documented this with respect to people in the past, who young children are ready to label as 'silly' on account of their different cultures. Besides, geography – like religious education – often depends upon *telling* children about other peoples, leading to some practitioners adopting a didactic way of working. In addition, children have to learn a set of symbols for describing other places in the form of maps. 'Piagetian' research has often showed that preschoolers are hopeless at it and that older children are little better. Lastly, if geography is understood as facts to be learned, and some parts of the national curriculum give such an impression, then it may be seen as demanding, sterile and threatening. On this view, discovery learning it isn't.

We recognize these fears but argue that they come in part from misapprehensions about early years geography. To repeat one of our themes, the way in which we understand subjects goes a long way in shaping practice. The view of geography presented above is not the only view.

While geography is about adults, it may also be about children. That still leaves the fact that children in other places live in ways that our learners may readily find funny, silly or incomprehensible. To a degree, this is a fact of young (and old?) life. The response that geography is therefore unsuitable for young children has two faults. First, we might equally say that maths or reading are unsuitable because children find those subjects hard and make many mistakes. The proportion of seven-year-olds who understand what is entailed by taking seven from twenty-one is evidence for that. But you might reply that maths and reading are so fundamental that we have to pursue them, even at the cost of much incomprehension and, even, unhappiness. Geography, you might say, is not like that, so why scourge children needlessly with it? Our second point is that geography *is* like that. It is essential. In a democracy committed to beliefs in human rights, liberty and equality, intolerance of others is a cause for considerable concern, especially as Britain develops an identity as a part of Europe rather than as the leader of many dependent countries. There is evidence that racism, one manifestation of intolerance, may be identified in three-years-olds, and that the early years are good ones in which to shape empathy (Milner 1983). What we are saying, then, is that geography is important as a *human* subject in a humanistic society. It may carry difficulties with it, but no more so than other key subjects. We will suggest that in fact these difficulties have been exaggerated.

The awarenesses that we might be trying to form in early geography could be that:

◀ people in different places live differently;
◀ different does not mean stupid;
◀ people live and act as they do for understandable reasons, not because they are stupid;
◀ different peoples need to be studied on their own terms;
◀ other ways of life have their own value;
◀ we need to try and understand other ways of life.

This casts geography as a moral study with much in common with religious education, history and English. It does not exclude the more common ideas that children should learn to map, to do fieldwork and look for patterns in the environment. All of these, though, are subordinate to the focus on other lifestyles, their logic and our common humanity. One of the main concerns of geography will therefore be to build up a picture of what it is like to live in different places, recognizing, as far as possible, the way people may *feel* about different places.

How might we teach about distant peoples, whether they be the peculiar groups who live in London, or the exotic folk of Scotland or Germany? Some telling *is* appropriate and people who deny that are also denying the power of stories and tales. These have always been a prime way of communication and entertainment and ought to be used in geography too, always given that stories are worked on with the principles that we set out above in mind. Pictures provide another way of learning about other places. Often undervalued, pictures are sources that can be 'read' by non-readers, who can learn to extract considerable amounts of information and to make inferences. Artefacts and video are also important, as is classroom information technology. It can help to use the overlay keyboard here. With year 2 children, school texts, whose quality is much improved of late, may also be used, as long as they are used as a resource to supplement story and picture, not to replace them.

What place is there in this for discovery learning? Plainly, any 'discovery' learning about distant peoples cannot be like that in mathematics, where children work on their immediate environments. Discovery learning is possible, though, if we treat it as providing plenty of resources, mainly in the form of pictures, and ask children to use them to shape a view of what distant children's lives are like. As with mathematics, we would want this discovery to take place within a structure provided by the teacher, to see group activity and to have conversations with children about why they come to certain conclusions. Play will be important, particularly role-play, as children begin to flesh out the meaning of leading a different life. We also see a place for practitioner exposition and storytelling. But without the discovery element, this geography could be too formal, dry and detached.

So far, we have been talking about the difficult case of incorporating developmentally appropriate activities into work on children of distant places. We have done that because we value the way that geography can extend children's horizons, which we see as a fundamental job of education. In reality, many practitioners are likely to dwell upon other forms of geography. If we look at the national curriculum in 1994, we see that children will work on the locality, as they will in history, learn about weather and about physical geography in the shape of soils and rocks. This links geography with a long tradition of environmental studies work that is characterized by practical and discovery work: about weather patterns, or on the differences in soil collected from different places, or on traffic patterns, or on litter. There is much that children can discover when geography is seen as a practical activity in finding out about the local environment, and all early years practitioners will have their own favourite activities. It is even possible, we suggest, for young children to make picture maps and in so doing discover the value of using a common set of symbols for features like houses, shops, roads, traffic lights etc.

We want to add a word of caution here. There is ample scope for learning through discovery in the locality but it is still important for teachers to structure these opportunities in ways that lead to useful geographical conclusions. That might be done through using a range of geographical questions along the lines of: 'Who goes to that place?' 'Why?' 'How do they get there?' 'Why do they use that way to get there?' 'Do you like that place (or spot)?' 'What do you like about it?' 'How could we make it better?' 'Do you think it was always like that?'

Geography can be tackled in ways that fit quite comfortably with notions of good early years practice. We recommend the use of photographs of visits to help children to place themselves in a situation and thereby initiate a process of joint remembering and discussion that can help them to build up the language they need to think and discuss within the discourse of geography.

Maps, though, are often seen as an exception to the rule that geography is compatible with beliefs about good early years practice. Modern research has, however, shown that children do know where some places are and can represent this in some form, although conventional, Ordnance Survey-style representations ought not to be expected. Children know much more about place than they can represent, and it is their difficulties in showing what they know that have led some commentators to assume that they don't actually have much grasp of place. But since most young children do have a knowledge of place, an important goal of early geography might be to give them a scaffolding to help them to become better at describing place through map-like work. Catling's (1990) list of thirty-seven ways of doing this can be recommended.

Geography, we conclude, is in a sense and at some level within children's grasp. Since it does not demand developmentally inappropriate teaching methods, we see no case for saying that geography is, in principle, beyond young children. In that much geography demands active discovery and practical work, we think it is a splendid resource for early years education. And because work on people in distant places is important to children's fragile awareness of what it is to be human, we think it is a necessary study.

History and the place of knowledge in the early years curriculum

We need to clarify what we have in mind by 'knowledge'. We want to distinguish between (1) knowing concepts, (2) knowing procedures (that is to say, having skills) and (3) knowing information or facts. The first two are fundamental. There are also relatively few skills and concepts to worry about. Subjects, as we have said, are one way of describing what the most important skills and concepts are, although we mustn't forget those associated with the social curriculum. Information comes in truckloads. It would be insensitive to the nature of young children to expect them to know lots of information or facts. Their memories hold a limited selection of unpredictable information for typically rather short periods of time. Furthermore, many ideas elude them. Lastly, their interests are distinctly childish, or infantile, and their attention span *tends* to be short. Teaching them geography or history and expecting them to store much detail would be fruitless, even callous. Instead, we need to isolate the concepts and skills that really matter and concentrate on helping children to master them, as we have indicated in the discussions of maths, religious education, science and geography. Children may remember the most unexpected clutter of information but the purpose of early years education is not to concentrate on this surface feature of learning. It is the conceptual and procedural bases of subjects that matter.

Let us develop this idea by looking at early years history. History is about stories and as such it fits well with young children's taste for the exotic and their attachment to story format. Talking about history stories can begin to develop awareness that people in the past were people much like us (and stories of people of other cultures and in other places can show that different peoples today are, nevertheless, people). Some 'time markers' can be put in, beginning a map of time past (and yes, there will be confusions and errors: much as there are with number, letters, rules, and so on). Children can talk about, handle, draw, model, arrange and play with objects from a part of the past (when their grandparents were young) and they can be encouraged to look for differences, to express preferences and to speak about change, albeit crudely. A key message is that we find out about the past through 'leftovers', through sources of all sorts. If we want to know what it was like, or what happened, we search for leftovers. Notice that history has its own possibilities for discovery learning.

This is what we mean by knowledge and awareness. From such work a time map is begun. Learners acquire, we hope, a general awareness that there is a past and that it is different; that different parts of the past differ from each other; that therefore things change over time; that people lived in the past and we can talk about stories about them much as we can talk about other stories. History is about trying to make sense of the leftovers to get a better picture of what it was like *then* and what happened. In the process, children will have acquired some factual knowledge – where their parents were born, how washing was done 40 years ago, what sort of things the Romans wore, that children used to write on slates and there were no computers, and so on. However, it is the awareness which matters. The details are decorations.

What we are saying, then, is that the knowledge which we are looking for in the early years is not factual knowledge as detail, but a knowledge of some of the basic ideas of a subject which has been developed through work on that subject. It is not crucial if a child forgets about Julius Caesar (and Claudius was more significant for British history anyway), or believes that there were motorways in Britain 50 years ago – these are matters of detail. They are rather like imagining that the Normans introduced the feudal system, that Mary I was bloodthirsty, or that General Custer had a 'last stand'. What does matter is that the work which children do is organized to instil a handful of key concepts and procedures drawn from a subject. The national curriculum attainment target statements go some way to describing these awarenesses but they suffer from two weaknesses. The lesser of the two is that the list is not always full enough, while the main one is that the attainment targets were not drawn up with early years children very much in mind. To only have statements at levels 1 and 2 to describe the learning which has taken place by the age of seven is far too crude. We need statements at level 0.5 – and perhaps at level 0.33 and 0.66 too – although this is straining the mathematical metaphor too far.

Let us develop this idea by looking at historical time. It is an old gibe that children have no sense of historical time. But adults don't necessarily understand time either. A President of the Historical Association has said that he doesn't understand the concept of a century, although he could define it. Time is a subjective experience that is measured objectively. We can only go some way to understanding our own and other people's subjective experiences but we can go a long way to mastering the objective system of measurement. If we break the concept into its components, we can identify a number of ideas which are manageable: that there has been a past; that there is an order to that past; that parents' youth came after grandparents' youth; that the two times were distinctive; that they differed from each other and from now; that we can add other time-markers to this elementary, three-point timeline; and that the sequence of these time-markers needs to be learned. Time, seen like that, is comprehensible and teachable in the early years.

The basic ideas about this system are that it is a way of defining the sequence of events, of showing the order in which things happen. It also allows us to put things in sets, identifying what things belong with what. For example, this idea of *contemporaneity* means that given a set of objects or postcards showing things from a few patches of time with which we are familiar, we could sort them into a Roman set, a Prehistoric set, a granny's set and a today set. The basis of the formal system of time is sequence and setting. Quite appropriate for young children. The number of time is the root of the idea that children cannot handle time. What is often meant is that they get the maths wrong, or have a faulty concept of a century or of a decade. The fact that they have no business doing that sort of work on the formal system of time, unless they choose to and are capable of doing so, seems to have been widely overlooked. Time is not dates. Dates are a precise way of indicating sequence and setting. They come *after* children have got working skill with those concepts. A fuller discussion with some examples is to be found in Knight (1991). So following the principles discussed earlier, we can distinguish between information – in this case dates – which is not the concern of practitioners, and the central concepts of sequence and contemporaneity, which are.

Time is not a problem. Nor is the idea of historical sources. History is an interpretation based on the leftovers of the past. Often there are no surviving sources and we just don't have an answer to questions like 'Who lived here a hundred years ago?', 'How many poor people were there here at the time of the gunpowder plot?', 'What was the purpose of Hadrian's Wall?' (not as obvious as is usually assumed). The sources that have survived have irritating habits, like being in Latin or illegible English, written for well-educated adults used to a certain style, being hard to understand, and being bitty and incomplete. Too hard for young children.

The simple answer is that this idea, that history is about making sense of leftovers, can be developed using accessible sources: buildings, people's memories in the form of oral history, pictures, artefacts and simple – or simplified – written sources. The principle of discovering the past from leftovers can be demonstrated in a developmentally appropriate, playful way.

Just as geography may involve looking at more distant peoples, so history entails some work on people beyond living memory, people who probably did not live locally. Story is the answer. The story of Robin Hood, for example, is not only a strong theme for all types of creative and aesthetic work, but also offers a powerful way to establish in children's minds an image of a period in the past, the Middle Ages (Knight 1992). As with geography, we see these stories as ways of engaging children in thought, imagination and feeling, not as excuses for didactic teaching.

The case of Robin Hood is well chosen, since not only is it debatable whether Robin ever existed, let alone robbed, but it is uncertain when he might have lived (but *definitely* not in the days of King Richard and King John) and where (probably not in Sherwood). This shows that history is not as much about facts as people sometimes suppose, and points us in the direction of saying that history, like geography, is about developing awareness of key ideas like sequence, contemporaneity, sources, people and their ways of life. Without going so far as to say that history and geography are about interpretations, so that you cannot make mistakes or be wrong, which is nonsense, we can emphasize that both are about imagination and interpretation. It is hard to see why either, in some respectable form, are beyond young children if we free ourselves from a concern to make sure children remember plenty of information. It is easy to believe that each subject is an important activity, being people-centred and carrying important ideas about differences in human affairs.

Technology, re-presentation and progression

There is a lot of redundancy in learning. By this we mean that it may take several attempts before we grasp something and that it will then take a lot of practice before we become confident or skilled with it. In earlier chapters, we identified two ways in which progress happens in learning. One is the way that a child encounters new information and then may restructure his or her thinking to accommodate to it. After that there should be consolidation work in the form of problem-solving and application tasks, which then give way to practice activities, designed to 'tune' performance. In this model, progress is associated with different sorts of task. This is compatible, as we have said, with a Vygotskian model, where progress is a case of learning to do something with support and with others and becoming steadily more autonomous to the point where no support is needed and the task can be done alone.

To these two models we have added a third. Jerome Bruner described learning as a spiral. As we move upwards in ever-wider swoops, we are gaining in conceptual understanding or skill and attaching more information to it. If we apply this spiral to any one procedure, such as designing, then we can see that the essential skill is the same, but that it also becomes steadily more sophisticated and associated with more and more information about designing. We can draw on the previous two models and say that these explain how we progress upwards and outwards, with tasks and social organization providing the impetus for this journey. The model of the spiral curriculum explains where we are going. It also tells us that we shall use the same procedures and concepts again and again. The important thing is that, over many years, we use them in more complex and sophisticated ways. We can see, then, that children aged four, six and eight might all design and build a model that goes fast or is a Lego room. It will not simply be repetition if practitioners have used the intervening years to move children along the spiral through an appropriate mixture of tasks and social settings.

Subjects, such as technology, are made up of key concepts and procedures that are to be developed in this fashion and which will be applied again and again, often to similar problems and similar situations. The test of its educational value is whether talk at the age of seven about the bicycle as a system is more insightful than talk at the age of five. This is how we understand Bruner's position that any subject can be taught to any child. It was not his claim that five-year-olds can become mini-geographers or mini-engineers. In all respects, their work would not just be inferior to mature geography and engineering, but also quite different from it. What he was driving at was the idea that they could begin to gain, crudely, some of the principles of geography or technology. In other words, strip a subject – or an issue – down to its core, to its simplest characteristic ideas, and then develop those ideas by constantly revisiting them.

Popularly, technology is taken to be routine problem solving using machinery and mathematical formulae. The ideas of machinery, of fixed methods and of correct solutions dominate this view of technology. While it is not entirely wrong, it is not the way that technology has been conceived for Key Stage 1 of the national curriculum (DES 1990b). Children are, indeed, to learn to use tools and materials safely, and in doing so to learn about their properties. But that is also true of art, for example. In technology, they are to observe and notice the world around them (as in art); to describe their products and solutions to others, evaluating both their own and others' solutions and refining them in the light of those evaluations (which is the same as for art).

The difference between art and technology is in the nature of the products. In art, the idea is to use techniques and skills to communicate a vision. Technology is also about vision, but in technology we are interested in envisioning and testing solutions to problems that exist in life. In art, the problem is how best to communicate a view of something, real or imaginary. In technology, the problem is to solve a problem. That, according to Attainment Target 2, involves generating and discussing proposals (which might also be done in art), and researching the market (which would not usually be a part of art work). A concern with systems is also a feature of technology. To quote the example in the national curriculum, children might be asked to examine a bicycle, to examine the different parts (sub-systems) and how they all relate to make the complete machine.

Were we to ask them which is the best bike, we might move into fair testing to see which can go the fastest. Ask which looks best and this is art. Ask which is the most useful for a variety of activities and we return to technology.

We are rather anticipating our forthcoming discussion of the degree to which a subject-led early years curriculum can still support an integrated, topic approach. We've done that because the links between technology and art are too strong to be ignored simply because the main focus of this section is on the re-presentation of problems. But now we return to that, beginning, true to our overall case, by identifying a distinctive element of early years technology. It was not well brought out in the 1990 version of the curriculum. Technology involves asking how things work, what powers them, and involves producing working solutions to problems. Children will therefore produce models or machines to do things using Lego, other construction systems, materials such as card or paper, and perhaps soft wood offcuts too. So we can see that materials and problems are likely to remain fairly similar across children's period of early years learning. How is progression to be achieved when there is so much re-presentation?

We suggest that a powerful answer can be got from assessment theory. Practitioners are familiar with norm-referenced assessment, where we are ranked against our peers as first, last or average. They also know about criterion-referenced assessment through having to match children's performances against national curriculum attainment targets. Criterion-referenced assessment does offer a way of putting progression into technology work, since it suggests targets for children to work towards as they develop. Of more interest to us is the related notion of ipsative assessment. This means comparing what a child can do *now* compared with what was achieved *then*. The child provides her or his own benchmark. What she or he could do is the standard against what she can do is to be measured. This thinking is very close to that which underpins records of achievement, which have been used with some success in Key Stage 1, and is clearly compatible with Vygotskian views on the zone of proximal development, outlined in Chapter 3.

We suggest that one way of building development into children's technology work is to keep work that they have done and to give it to them a year later with the brief to evaluate its good points and to identify things that they could improve. The task is then to improve on the earlier effort. By quite literally re-presenting technology to children, we can find a powerful way of encouraging them along the spiral of progression.

Music, re-presentation and progression

Music is akin to physical education in that there are strong aesthetic elements and there is also a set of physical techniques to be mastered. These should

ideally be practised but it is hard to see how school time for regular practice might be found. It is likely, therefore, that the goal will be a general
awareness of music, like art, as a form of communication and expression.
Consequently, we might expect similar principles to apply, and indeed,
according to the national curriculum, they do (DES 1992b).

Children need to perform and compose music. Performance will
usually be expressed through singing, rhythmic work, and perhaps a pitched
instrument such as the recorder. They will learn something of the range of
sounds that may be made by different instruments and to play an instrument [which may be a rhythm instrument, such as tambourine, xylophone,
triangle, maracas or sound boxes and scrapers (made in technology?)] in
some fashion. This playing should lead towards them organizing sounds
purposefully to illustrate a poem, story or mood. They will also see that
performance can be stored and planned through a system of symbols to
represent it. This need not demand work on the formal system of musical
notation. There is a clear parallel with emergent writing where children use
their own ways of recording a piece of music.

Progression in these performance-related aspects of music is usually
said to come from practice, although children are unlikely to get a great
deal of practice in school, save in singing, perhaps. There is also progression through greater understanding and insight. As children learn more
about instruments and playing, they are able to tackle any given task with
greater resources to call upon. Listening to music and talking about its feel
and effect is also a way to promote progression.

This will often mean listening to their own performances and talking about how these might be improved. It should also lead to them listening to polished works in a variety of genres, from a variety of cultures,
including 'classical ' music, folk, pop and non-Western music. As with art,
the idea is that there is a variety of styles of expression, with the range of
musical instruments being analogous to the range of materials available to
the artist. This might be done by listening to different ways of representing
similar emotions, or to different ways of conveying sounds around them
– the noises of animals, of traffic, and of open countryside, for example.
Music from different times and places will probably be used. As with art,
technology and physical education, judgement and discussion are involved,
both influencing subsequent planning and performance. We recognize that
this aspect of the music curriculum is more problematic than performing
music. As with reading, it will often not come easily. As with reading,
substantial experience is called for. Unlike reading, music is not seen as a
high-priority subject. It is hard to see how to resolve this. Perhaps a coping strategy is to accept that programmes should be ambitious, as in the
national curriculum, but that exigencies may mean that attainments are
modest. Again, then, we are suggesting that developing a musical awareness
in children that allows some operation within the discourse as listener,
performer and composer is the aim.

Where practitioners are clear about the awarenesses that they are fostering and have a concept of how they might develop, then similar musical problems and similar musical ideas can be usefully re-encountered across the early years.

English and the integrated curriculum

English, like mathematics, is one of the priorities for early years education identified in the Dearing Report (1993). It is also an extensive and complicated area of the curriculum. While it demands that practitioners have specialist knowledge in order to create the most productive classroom engagements, it fits well into an integrated approach to the curriculum, as the Dearing Report acknowledges. If a broad curriculum is to be planned for children, the time can only be made available by making sure that some tasks are carrying two subjects at once. English is involved in everything children do in the early years and it is no exaggeration to say that children read and write more outside English 'lessons' than they do within them. This means that children do geography and English, technology and English, art and English. As the Bullock Committee (1975) stated, language needs to be learned, taught and appraised across the curriculum and it is best learned in a context that gives a purpose to the learning.

We will look at aspects of English teaching before returning to the issue of integration.

Talk
Wells (1986) argued that in classrooms children tended to be swept along by teachers' 'brisk efficiency'. Opportunities for them to plan and reflect through exploratory talk were limited, he said. At school they speak with fewer adults than at home, ask fewer questions, initiate fewer conversations, use less complex utterances and express a narrower range of meanings than they do outside school. Adults at school were half as likely as other adults to incorporate children's meanings by extending them or by getting children to do so. These young children were cast into passive roles in school conversations with adults. His evidence includes the example of a group which had visited Berkeley Castle and then 'discussed' four-poster beds. This silliness does highlight the fact that we all too easily call things discussion that are nothing of the sort – they are sessions where practitioners hear various children speak individually while the rest listen. The teacher approves some of their points and politely ignores others. This is audience participation in the teacher's exposition. It is nothing like discussion. So in the case of the castle, children's reactions to the visit were excluded from this rather bizarre follow-up. As Wells observed, 'discussion' with the whole class invariably made most of them listeners. The objection to talk governed by such a teacher agenda is 'not that teachers try to extend children's knowledge, but that they try so hard to do so that they never really discover what it is about the child's experience that he or she finds sufficiently

interesting to want to share in the first place' (Wells 1986: 89). Moreover, it does little for children's language use and language learning.

Yet, Wells said, children do come to school with robust oral language abilities that are sufficient for them to progress with reading and writing. Unfortunately, oral work and activities seemed to feature less in the curriculum from year 1 onwards. This might be because of the pressures, which we have said that we regard as illegitimate, to emphasize formal instruction. There is also a tendency to have children write so much.

Talk needs to be valued in all subjects and for all ages. Even the national curriculum, not normally seen as a liberal document, has the attainment target of listening and speaking. But what sort of talk?

We want to distinguish between talk and chatter. Talk is purposeful within a learning setting, unlike chatter. Chatter can be a classroom problem, unlike talk. We might aim to improve children's confidence as talkers, their clarity, ability to use standard English when appropriate, and their skills in discussion. Drama and role-play should both be apparent. They ought also to learn to advance a point of view. The obvious question at this point is what should they talk about? This is where the idea of a broad curriculum is so valuable, since the subjects that make it up provide plentiful opportunities for talk of all sorts.

Reading

Plainly we want children to learn to read. We add two qualifications. One is that it is important for them to enjoy reading, much as we saw with maths. This has implications for the way in which reading is learned. A central argument for the 'real books' approach, eloquently set out by Waterland (1988), is that it is not nearly as dull as the reading schemes that she regards as sterile, hence as fatal to children's love of reading. As we suggested in Chapter 2, and in the section on mathematics, an important aim of early years education is that children should encounter subjects without becoming deterred and disheartened. That can easily lead to children being labelled as poor learners or failures, which easily leads to entrenched alienation from education. Failure leads to frustration, lack of effort and often to misbehaviour (after all, what else is there to do?), and these reinforce the failure, which leads to a further loss of motivation.

Our second qualification is that it is possible to read without reading. In the early stages, it is quite possible to mistake the faltering ability to sound out words for understanding. Often, though, children learn to 'bark at print'. This is not reading. As the national curriculum makes clear (DES 1990c), reading is thinking about print to make sense of it. And making sense involves sensitivity to style and language, as well as the ability to use contents and indexes, and to skim and scan when appropriate. Reading, then, is a complex and sophisticated art, requiring a curriculum geared to doing much more than getting children to sound out words.

'Poor work', said HMI (1991: 6), 'is not strongly associated with any particular method of teaching reading. It appears to have much more to do with inadequate planning; unsound management and organization of the teaching and learning; inconsistencies in applying teaching methods, and poor assessment of children's progress'. In an earlier report, they had associated good teaching with the provision of a good range of reading materials; with creating opportunities for unfragmented reader–adult contact; and with a link between reading and writing. While they thought that some systematic teaching of phonics was also associated with higher standards (HMI 1990: 7), they did not see that phonics was a better way of teaching reading than the 'real books' approach – both are necessary.

That is not the view taken by some commentators on the evidence that the standard of children's reading has deteriorated in recent years. For them, it was neglect of phonics and the prevalence of 'real books' that were to blame. There *has* been a decline in scores on reading tests in some local education authorities, and while it is tempting to blame the curriculum, the link with a 'real books' curriculum cannot be made. While there is a better case for arguing that phonics do need to be taught quite systematically, we also notice research that shows that poverty is correlated with poor school performance and that points to the growth of poverty in recent times, not least in the areas which have reported declines in reading scores. That is not to imply that schools are powerless in the face of poverty, for there is increasingly convincing evidence that schools *do* differ in the extent to which they help children's academic progress. But even good schools are limited in what children from poorly resourced homes achieve, on average.

The moral for the reading curriculum is plain. It should be varied, not Victorian and narrow. It should also be a priority in reading, as in all subjects, to help children see why they are doing it. This can start in the under-fives years. Wells (1986: 159) argued that:

> If some children make little progress in learning to read and write, the problem, as we observed it, was not that they had insufficient oral language resources, but that they had not yet discovered the purpose of reading or writing or the enjoyment to be gained from these activities . . . For them, what is required is one-to-one interaction with an adult centred on a story.

Clearly, this is especially important for the under-fives, although we must avoid making the mistake of supposing that it is not important for older children.

A further point is that because reading pervades the curriculum, an audit ought to be done of the reading that children do normally, as a part of their daily work in maths, geography, art and the like. We believe that it would show that older children spend most of their reading time on 'transactional' reading, as opposed to reading for pleasure and in order to extend their range of reading abilities. This is serious, since it means that whatever view practitioners have of the reading curriculum, if it doesn't also take account of all the reading children do for other subjects, there will be a considerable mismatch between what the practitioner believes is going on and what children experience. It wouldn't be surprising if some were fed up with reading, even though the teacher had a good policy for reading within 'English time'. By the same reasoning, audits are also useful for the writing curriculum.

Integration, then, is not unambiguously a good idea. With reading and writing integration can frustrate practitioners' subject-specific aims by overlaying them with the demands of reading and writing to service other work. The solution is to bring those reading and writing activities into the view of the English curriculum and to apply the same principles to them as to work that is labelled 'English', pure and simple. The moral is that integration needs to be based on careful thinking about how subject interests are to be preserved and not lost by a topic approach. Topics can damage the teaching of reading and writing. They need not, but that is most likely to happen where thought has been given to how reading and writing will be developed through topics.

Writing

What we have said of reading largely holds true for writing too. An enormous amount of school writing is pointless rubbish, promoting a corrosive dislike of writing in young children. One of the best ways of developing effective English work would be to do an audit of the writing that children have to do and then get rid of the work that is there basically to keep children occupied.

Why write?

As for art – for pleasure and to communicate. Writing is also a useful aid to thought, acting as a record of information and of earlier thoughts. It is both instrumental and creative. It follows, then, that the curriculum ought to prepare children in the mechanics of writing, but it should also help them to see that writing has a variety of purposes and can take a variety of forms.

Of teaching children the mechanics of writing we will say little. This is well covered in a number of books, showing the importance of supporting children's emergent literacy and of fostering a positive attitude (that point again) to writing. Practice, work on the mechanics of spelling without being obsessive about developing children's visual memories, all follow. As do the recognition and eventual use of the basic rules of punctuation. Increasingly, the importance of drafting and redrafting, involving talking about writing, is being acknowledged. Unfortunately, few schools have enough personal computers for the purpose, and notepad word-processors (retailing at £102 at the time of writing) are not much used in years 1 and 2. We also fear that redrafting is often seen by children as a tidying-up operation, concentrating on grammar, presentation and spelling. More direct teaching about the ways in which redrafting can improve the quality or aesthetics of prose is needed, much as analogous work is needed in art, technology, music, and so on. We do not mean that this teaching will simply be didactic. Discussion, experiment and evaluation with a sense of purpose and audience in mind are likely to be more effective.

This has taken us to the purposes of writing. In auditing current writing practices, practitioners should have in mind the variety of audiences, purposes and styles of writing and be looking for opportunities to associate them with work in other subjects. This analysis is not just an aid to balance, but also makes it plain where some purposes and audiences are best served through separate English work.

Special needs and the English curriculum

Work by Blatchford (1990, 1991), building on the work of Tizard and colleagues (1988), has shown that children who on entry to school are able to sound out and name letters are more likely to score well on reading tests at age seven. Similarly, a handwriting test is a good predictor of writing skills at age seven. If this is so, he suggests, then teachers might use these findings to identify children at risk of falling well behind by the age of seven. As we have said, it appears that keeping children from special educational provision is a worthwhile and rewarding achievement. We offer no additional advice on how such children are to be taught, not least because our general stance is that good education is good education – the principles that apply to good teaching for most children are those that should also serve the strongest and weakest performers. Hegarty (1987: 169) expressed this as 'how does one distinguish between carefully planned teaching geared to the individual needs of each pupil and special provision conceived as something additional?' A similar line is taken in the collection edited by Ainscow (1991). A special initiative to help children with special educational needs is the reading recovery programme, which has had ministerial support and promised to do much to redeem reading failures. There is plenty of evidence that it is effective. We suggest that early years teachers who work with children who have these special needs might be helped by looking at the programme in some detail. However, it is an expensive programme, requiring a lot of highly skilled individual attention for each failing reader, as well as home support. The costs have been justified by showing how much greater are the costs of special needs provision for children whose reading does not recover from a poor start. While this is true, those are costs to the system. It is unlikely that without additional finance schools would be able to adopt reading recovery approaches. Nonetheless, practitioners are likely to find the principles helpful (Wade 1992; Wright 1992).

Integration and English

English is not typical of the scope that exists for retaining an integrated curriculum while planning around subject discourses. English is so widely used that the bigger problem is in making sure that its key concerns are not swamped by its service role. In part our answer has been that audits need to be done across the curriculum as the first stage in countering that. Another part of our answer is that when thinking about the variety of reading, writing, talking and listening activities that are implied by effective education in English, deliberate attempts need to be made to distribute those tasks across the curriculum. By all means let English serve other subjects, but let them also serve English by providing good contexts for effective English learning.

Art and the integrated curriculum

Seen as a broad subject, understood as the promotion of awarenesses, and taught with alertness to talk and judgement making, art can be seen as a fundamental activity. When we are thinking about young children who have little grasp of writing, then art, or in Bruner's terms, 'iconic representation', will be a form of communication second only to talk and play. It ought, therefore, to pervade the curriculum. Following that line leads to a reappraisal of where art does appear in children's experience of school. We suggest that a lot more pictorial representation takes place than is contained in art lessons, and that this shows how art is naturally integrated into much early years learning and that more opportunities exist for children to work artistically than is often recognized.

In this case, then, adopting a subject-centred approach to the curriculum has the power to raise our awareness of the possibilities that there are for working with young children without corralling us into a timetable that has a ghetto called art within it. Yet these possibilities depend for their fruition on practitioners being clear themselves about the awarenesses they are hoping to nurture and on the set of ways of so doing. Art, on this view, cannot be taken as a 'filler' activity to do mainly with painting. Such misapprehensions might be better associated with curriculum forms that are not grounded in subject understandings.

Art is about helping children to express their observations, feelings and fantasies through a variety of media. Not only is it a form of communication, it is also a way of refining the way we see the world. Picasso said that 'people must be forced to see painting in spite of nature. We always believe that we're looking, right? But it's not true. We're always looking through glasses' (quoted by Gardner 1983: 199). The awarenesses that art could promote, then, would be observational and interpretative. Children ought to grow in the understanding that artistic creations communicate all sorts of things, from photo-like representations, to evocations of mood and other feelings; that stories can be told and situations represented; and that art may be pleasurable as an activity and as a product. Associated with that are discussions, evaluations, descriptions and talk in general about art works. Art, then, is not only a way of communication; it ought also to be the subject of communication, a matter for thought, feeling and interchange. And, lastly, art is thought, although we would not go as far as Kellogg (1979: 5), who claimed that 'only free drawing, fully appreciated by adults, allows for the mental activity that interests the child at the moment, and this spontaneous work is the best stimulus for individual work that is mind-building'.

The art aspect of the curriculum ought, then, to convey the message that art is a way of sharing experience and imagination with others. It is a social activity, to be talked about. It is a technical activity, and education is partly to do with enlarging the palette of techniques that may be used to express feelings and ideas. Skill-building is important in art and it is interwoven with the development of concepts – concepts such as balance, colour and the limits, as well as the potential, of different media. It is an individual activity as well, personal but public; to do with feelings and thought. None of this is inappropriate to young children, always given that we accept that children's representations are constrained by their technical ability as well as by a documented developmental sequence that affects the way that children try to depict things.

The national curriculum (DES 1992a) requires children in years 1 and 2 to be investigating and making. Typical activities involve observing and recording, perhaps by using different grades of pencils – lenses too, if need be – to record their close observation of historical artefacts or other stimulus pieces. Collections of children's work are to be organized (but not necessarily mounted or displayed) by them. If children were doing work on the locality, then collections might be compiled of rubbings from different sites; of sketches of windows or door furniture; of different colours seen in roofing and building materials; or of photographs of key sites, involving groups of children in discussing what ought to be included, where and why.

Their representations should be in a variety of media – textiles, clay, collages, paints, pen and pencils, for example – and in three as well as in two dimensions. They will need not just to explore these media but also to learn about possibilities. Children's drawing can advance considerably if they are taught about the different effects that can be achieved by different grades of pencil, and about smearing and shading. Lest we be misunderstood, it should be said that revealing the potential of different media goes in harness with giving children plentiful opportunities to experiment with those techniques. Nor is discovery to be derided. Making different materials available and asking children to use whichever they choose in order to create something 'scary' is a valuable art activity when it is accompanied by comparison and talk about the effects. Opportunities to rework the creations in the light of class talk are to be provided.

The importance of talk in art has been alluded to, and it is especially important for the second attainment target, entitled 'knowledge and understanding'. Children should see, and more importantly talk about, works of art from different times and different places, representing different styles. They might also try to emulate the feel or the effect of a piece of work that appeals to them.

It has been alleged that this might amount to an inappropriate art history and art appreciation course, but we see no reason why this should be. Talking about and responding to art is quite different from being told what is good art and learning about great artists. It is about sharing reactions, making choices and explaining those choices: it is about becoming aware that there are many ways of conveying ideas and feelings, using many styles and many media. As Sedgwick and Sedgwick (1993) note, learning is not about learning the right responses to great art – to believe that is to misunderstand completely what art is about.

Dawn and Fred Sedgwick's *Drawing to Learn* (1993) can be commended as a thoughtful, experience-based account of ways of teaching some aspects of art to young children. Not only do they discuss many techniques but they are also good at showing how art work links with other parts of the curriculum, English and technology for example, and how it is an approach to cross-curricular themes such as the diversity of human culture, experience and belief.

In this section, we have raised similar fears to those expressed in the section on English. It is not so much a problem of integrating art with other subjects as ensuring that art does not thereby become reduced to a service function with the result that its special concerns get lost. Integration, it appears, may be as much about preserving distinctiveness as about joining similarities.

Physical education and fitness and the integrated curriculum

If art and technology have many ways of working in common but are separated principally by their purpose (communication and self-expression in one case, practical problem-working in the other), then physical education (PE) is linked to both by some elements of its ways of working, for the national curriculum (DES 1992c) also calls for children to plan, to work on problems and to evaluate their performances and solutions. There is also a strong link with art through dance – Gardner combines the two in his category of 'spatial intelligence'.

Dance, with its overt aesthetic goals is but one part of PE. The American Alliance for Health, Physical Education, Recreation and Dance identifies the following areas of activity for early years children (AAHPERD 1991): gym (which should not be formal); games (but not team games); dance (but not performance); and aquatics (if possible). All of these activities should contribute to the affective domain (the realm of feelings and attitudes) by, for example, building confidence, encouraging collaboration, responsibility and independence. Furthermore, 'physical activity . . . is also a laboratory for many types of cognitive learning' (p. 23). So far, it is unlikely that this account of the subject would cause early years teachers to worry. More contentious is AAHPERD's insistence that children need to be active throughout PE work, so that 'it is simply not acceptable to place children in long lines waiting to take turns, to seat them in circle games with only one or two children moving' (p. 21). Underlying their position is concern for the health of the nation, based on evidence of unhealthy diets and passive lifestyles. Unsurprisingly, they allocate to their members a considerable responsibility for health education, saying that 'the direct teaching of health as a separate subject must receive priority as the best method of providing health instruction' (p. 28). We will address health education later in this chapter.

Having seen that some Americans are happy with the idea of PE as a separate subject, we turn to the English national curriculum's description of it, which is actually quite similar. The main areas are athletics (which is not named in the American proposals, but which is clearly covered in their description of appropriate activities, which includes running, jumping, sliding, hopping, striking, throwing and kicking); gym; dance; games (which does not mention team games, but perhaps implies them); outdoor activities; and swimming as an option.

We suggest that there are two substantial problems with PE in the early years. The first, by no means trivial, is practical. Not only are many early years institutions short of facilities (indoor and outdoor), making it hard to provide enough PE, but it is also a very time-consuming subject. Practitioners do not need reminding of children's difficulties dressing themselves and how much time it takes. As we shall see, in Key Stage 1 the day is taken up with the 'basics' and practical, time-consuming, expensive work is pushed to the edges (Campbell *et al.* 1992). It is hard to see how a worthwhile programme of PE and fitness can be secured by one harried session a week. We will return to the time issue at the end of this chapter.

The second problem relates to the identity of PE. We understand that it is an occasion for children to run, jump, prance and let off steam. Time needs also to be given over to the aesthetics of movement; to developing a fairly well-defined set of physical skills, whose levels of difficulty are progressively raised; and to keeping children active in the interests of fitness. Unless practitioners have these ideas to the fore, PE can fail as a subject just as art fails if art is reduced to simple painting in order to free time for practitioners to do 'demanding' subjects with other children. In other words, PE does not have to be integrated with other subjects for it to be in danger of becoming bland activity, shorn of its special concerns.

The question of how PE might be integrated with other topics is the wrong way round. It is hard, for example, to see how PE might be fitted into history or technology. Integration is possible but it needs to be approached the other way around, by taking worthwhile PE activities and asking whether there are valid opportunities to include elements of other subjects in them. Obviously language possibilities arise, mathematics ones too. There are also links with biology. If we want to go much beyond that, it is possible, we suppose, but the curse of integration then rises up: it is the danger of making contrived and bogus connections in order to make a topic, rather than have to manage some subject themes in isolation. While it would be possible to do history and geography in association with football, we think it's a thoroughly bad idea, leading to poor geography and poor history. The limits to integration need to be as clearly understood as the possibilities.

Summary: subjects and the integrated curriculum

Subjects are organized accounts of the nature of knowledge. There are other ways of organizing knowledge, around problems for example. However, we have taken the subject perspective since it is well-established and represented by the national curriculum. Subjects have their own discourses, directing attention to their own concerns, concepts and ways of working. Their concepts and concerns are often not shared by other subjects, although there is an overlap within humanities and social sciences, within natural sciences and between aesthetic subjects. Their procedures, skills or ways of working are shared to a much greater extent, although they do not invariably overlap.

So even if our starting point is planning in terms of subjects, there is considerable potential for planned integration. We will still need to recognize when a subject's perspectives cannot be properly conveyed by an integrated approach. The biggest criticism of topic work as it has been done, is that often distinctive subject perspectives have been overlooked and the integrity of subject knowledge and ways of knowing have become eroded.

In this chapter, we have pointed to some of the ways in which subjects can overlap with one another and interpenetrate. We suggest that canny curriculum planning might involve thinking about subject integration as something that may at least be possible, if not always achievable, at three different levels (Knight 1993):

◀ *By content*: several subjects can easily be joined to give a better view of a theme than could be achieved by separate subject approaches. An example would be joining art, geography and history in work on the immediate locality.
◀ *By shared skills or procedures*: an example would be joining the aesthetic subjects and English in a dramatized portrayal of, say, a story.
◀ *Through general thinking skills*: this is the hardest. It involves identifying thinking and working strategies that underlie most subjects and having a conscious school policy to develop them at every opportunity. We would aim to make children more aware of our preferred ways of thinking and working. Becoming aware of our own thought processes is sometimes known as metacognition and is seen as a promising approach to improving the quality of learning in schools, work and universities.

What we are saying, then, is that a subject-led approach to the curriculum need not lead to a timetable of entirely single-subject teaching. Nor, as we have repeatedly insisted, need it involve over-formal and inappropriate learning methods, let alone the pressure to work formally that can be so corrosive of children's sense of efficacy.

Cross-curricular themes

A subject-led curriculum does not tell the whole story, as the English government recognized in the 1988 Education Act. In this section, we shall briefly discuss some of the cross-curricular themes that also need space. We also need to say that it is for early years practitioners to add others, according to the values promoted by their organization and the context in which they work.

For example, the Dearing Report (1993) has made information technology (IT) into a cross-curricular theme. Children in years 1 and 2 will use IT for music-making, maths, writing and data-handling. Overlay keyboards are likely to be used to support writing, overcome children's unfamiliarity with the QWERTY keyboard, and to help children to 'read' pictures better. Art and IT are far from incompatible and many schools use graphics and paintbrush programmes with colour printers.

Some may doubt that IT is appropriate to preschool children, which we dispute. The overlay keyboard enables these children to choose pictorial representations and get a response from the screen and through the speaker, using voice synthesizing software. This opens up many possibilities for interactive learning, and learning the alphabet and letter sounds comes to mind as a powerful use, if that is an appropriate curriculum goal. Computers can also read text to children, albeit in the style of a dozy Dalek. Number recognition and simple number work may also be supported by the same technology.

And then there are arcade-type games. This is not normally seen as a part of education, which is quite understandable. However, even the more banal do a great deal to promote fine motor skills and hand–eye coordination, which are goals of the PE curriculum. Moreover, the more intelligent role-playing games make useful demands on children's reasoning powers, and where these games are played by a group, the quantity and quality of discussion can be a revelation. We do not wish to push these claims too strongly, not least because there is no evidence of which we are aware that skill at *Ultima Underworld II* transfers in the shape of supple thinking in the more conventional curriculum. We do wish to note that IT offers often-overlooked opportunities for play that may be seen as educationally worthwhile.

We have already talked about moral education in the context of RE. It should permeate other areas of the curriculum too. This strategy depends upon the observation that geography and history, for example, have strong moral overtones, may be vehicles for addressing environmental issues (how green is our valley?), and revolve around inter-cultural concerns. Health education, to take another example, might be located within PE and science. In planning the curriculum, practitioners would look for opportunities to work on the cross-curricular themes in the context of topics derived from the separate subjects. Given the common belief that children learn holistically, this integration of the curriculum has an appeal. It may be contrasted with 'bolt-on' planning for these themes, where children get separate, perhaps only occasional, lessons on cleaning their teeth, caring for others, switching off lights and not telling fibs.

However, a well-reported problem with teaching integrated topics is that children's normal uncertainty about what it is they are supposed to be learning, if anything, is juxtaposed with practitioners' difficulties in keeping sight of the many messages that go with combining many perspectives. In brief, integration can be the educational equivalent of Neapolitan ice-cream. In the tub, the three colours are distinguishable, but the product of mashing them together is a dun splodge.

The separatist approach of teaching cross-curricular themes as stand-alone topics is also deficient: first, because insufficient time tends to be made available and, second, because practitioners often lack the clarity of purpose and the support of teaching and learning materials that can contribute to effective education. Third, this separates the themes from the other school subjects, although the common claim that this is harmful is open to question.

Our position draws on both perspectives. Curriculum planning should identify points where moral, environmental, health and inter-cultural issues may be located in planning from a subject base. This is consistent with the integration of content which so many practitioners value and it also helps in identifying the web of 'big ideas' that defines the curriculum. However, not all of the things that matter about these four themes will be covered through subject-based planning, unless the subjects are twisted in the name of integration. We need to distinguish between the key notions of each theme, which ought to be raised through subjects, and important content, which might not be.

In discussing geography, we identified the key principles of inter-cultural understanding. Similar principles need to be identified for moral education, 'green' education and health education. These, we suggest, *can* be woven into the subject curriculum. Some of the content that schools might be expected to cover cannot. Bullying, theft, spitefulness, bottle banks, energy saving, avoiding slurryburgers, eating your greens, and helping others may be fitted into the story of Robin Hood, perhaps, but are better dealt with separately and in some cases as opportunities present themselves. These and other themes are, then, subject-like in that effective provision means that practitioners latch on to the 'big ideas' that underpin them and plan to see that these ideas are repeatedly encountered in the early years. Some of the associated content may be taught in integrated settings, as is the case with other subjects, but some will need to be taught separately, again as is the case with other foundation subjects. In effect, what we have done is expanded the list of foundation subjects.

The one hundred-and-fifty per cent curriculum?

Campbell and colleagues (1992) examined infant teachers' workloads as the national curriculum was washing into schools. Their findings are disturbing and could be taken to imply that our ideas on the early years curriculum are hopelessly idealistic. They found that teachers' experience was 'an enervating treadmill of hard work that rarely gave them a sense that they had achieved what they intended to do' (p. 153). Children were less frequently being heard reading and teachers were trying to identify some subjects as 'low-input' subjects that would free up time for other, demanding activities such as observation and assessment. And Campbell (1993: 25) said that 'at the very most, about fifteen minutes a day was left for each of the . . . foundation subjects and RE. Most of these subjects at Key Stage 1 are practical, time-consuming activities'.

One reaction would be to say that the curriculum ought to be pruned – emphasize the core subjects (of which more in the next chapter) and stop worrying about achieving a broad but impracticable curriculum. To people who see the goal of education as giving children a thorough grounding in the 'basics', this is appealing, and the Dearing Report (1993) seems to endorse this strategy. As Campbell noted, though, this goes against teachers' ideology, since early years practitioners do seem to be committed to a broad curriculum. Moreover, they have been critical, as we have seen, of over-pressured curricula and there is some evidence that children subjected to a curriculum stressing academic achievement do not flourish in their schooling.

Our resistance to this solution is partly based upon such evidence but also comes from our view of the purpose of education. It is, we aver, about much more than the three Rs. It is an enriching induction into knowledge and ways of working that are central to our cultures. As we have suggested, that means addressing central forms of experience, which are represented by national curriculum subjects and some other themes. However, can such a view survive the evidence that schools are hard pressed to cope?

We see some potential in what Campbell (1993) has described as an ameliorist position. That involves identifying opportunities for merging content, taking history and geography together through local studies for example. We have also suggested that if practitioners identify the key ideas and practices of subjects, then it is easier to advance them and not get bogged down in the clutter that is peripheral to the development of children's awarenesses of art, music, PE, geography and the like. Similarly, we can see scope for reducing the content of some prescriptions, whether that be done through the reforms of the Dearing review or through practitioners thinking in a more tough-minded fashion about what they want to cover with their children. In the preschool years, practitioners can do this without being hamstrung by the national curriculum. They also have the right, denied to teachers of older children, to do without religious education.

Yet these ideas hardly solve the problem. Approaching a solution involves doing what the Bullock and Cockcroft Committees recommended for the English and the mathematics curricula, and thinking about the teaching of these subjects across the curriculum. We think this is consistent with the Dearing proposals that these core subjects dominate the earliest years of schooling. We argue, though, that they can be taught to a very large extent through the broad curriculum that we advocate. If you take this line, that preschool learning is broad, that it is big ideas that underpin it and that happy engagement is more important than academic achievement, come what may, it is easier to see how the curriculum conundrum might be solved. Breadth is to be preferred over depth. It may be that in *these* six weeks we shall emphasize 'green' issues and in the *those* six weeks science-led work will prevail. It may well be that the need to provide children with room to play on materials of their choice and to provide good-quality care will mean that these young children may not do many 'green' topics. So be it. If the aim is to establish awareness and to shape attitudes, that may not matter very much. We would except PE from this formula, since fitness is something that does need to be worked at continuously.

Years 1 and 2 are more constrained. We are not convinced that it is serious if children do not get *continuous* experience of the foundation subjects. It is more important that they have more intensive experience of purposefully and playfully working within a subject framework. Education, we must remember, does not finish at the age of seven. Even at the age of eleven or sixteen or eighteen, people's detailed understandings are riddled with misapprehensions. What matters, we suggest, is that awarenesses of core ideas in a range of valued areas of human experience is steadily shaped. This purpose distinguishes education from development.

Effective curriculum: a summary

The main points we have made in these chapters on curriculum are:

1 We cannot talk of effective early years education without making it clear what we expect to be effectively achieved.
2 A broad curriculum ought to be planned for all.
3 Content should be selected to represent key forms of knowledge in our culture.
4 Here, subjects are important frameworks.
5 Practitioners need to be clear about the awarenesses that they are trying to form through the curriculum.

6 Play and practical work ought not to be compromised by such curriculum planning.

7 Subject integration is possible, although ambitious groupings can prove to be self-defeating.

8 Schools do make a difference to children's progress – what schools do matters.

9 Good schools and good teaching are good for *all* children, although not necessarily equally beneficial to all.

10 Care is an important part of early years provision and education.

11 Demarcations between school-based teachers and other early years workers are being eroded and there are signs that an integrated profession of early years workers may be emerging.

12 Yet schools cannot remedy society's problems, only ameliorate them somewhat – perhaps. Exaggerated claims rebound on practitioners.

13 The planned curriculum will not be faithfully created in practice, nor will all children construct exactly the understandings that practitioners intend.

14 Proposals to make the initial professional education of early years practitioners less extensive are palpable nonsense. We have described curriculum planning as a complex and sophisticated activity that demands extensive understanding of children, learning, teaching and curriculum theory.

Points for reflection

1 There has been interest in the idea of separating care from education. Writing of caring, Bereiter (1972) said that it was 'an abundance of things to do in and out of school that will make for a good life' (p. 407) 'without regard to the children getting anything in particular out of them' (p. 408). Which foundation subjects might contribute to such a programme of care? Why? What implications can you see for the education of 'carers'? What objections are there to making this the basis of *all* early years learning?

2 How does the curriculum of your institution compare to the one advocated thus far? If there are differences, what are they, why are they there, should anything be done, could anything be done, and how?

3 Can you reduce to a couple of curt sentences your ideas about the main business of each of the foundation subjects and themes? If not, why not? Does it matter?

4 Have we described a system that depends upon a curriculum coordinator system? If we have, is that a weakness in our suggestions? If not, what are the implications for the early years curriculum?

5 We have said that we could see a number of ways in which the 'developmental' view of early years education might be challenged. We did not, however, take up that challenge. Do you think it is sensible to question the assumption that the main aims of early years work is to promote development? And if the assumption is open to question, what difficulties can you see with that 'developmental' position?

6　Suppose that the content of the curriculum for years 1 and 2 were being reviewed. What labels should be given to the major blocks of work – should curriculum continue to be described in terms of subjects? What are the advantages of your preference over other ways of describing the curriculum for these years?

7　*Starting with Quality*, which is the title of a report of a government committee on the education of under-fives (DES 1990a), states that the principles guiding the Education Reform Act should also guide curriculum planning for younger learners. Those principles are that the curriculum should promote the physical, spiritual, moral, mental and cultural understanding of learners in a way that is fair to all, regardless of race, gender or religion. The curriculum should be broad and balanced and be conceived of in tandem with the business of caring for young children. How compatible is this with the curriculum that we have delineated? Does it make for a satisfactory curriculum?

Further reading

The HMI series *Teaching and Learning* . . . provides concise descriptions of their beliefs about effective practice in the foundation subjects. Of course, this is the 'party line' that is being rehearsed, and the series is not concerned with preschool children.

In the UK, there is little written about the content of early years curricula and the American sources we used are not easily accessible. A useful, recent overview is provided succinctly by David *et al.* (1992). It differs in several respects from the case we are developing. Equally, we are at odds with the work of Blenkin and Kelly, an example of which is contained in a brief review of the national curriculum (Kelly and Blenkin 1993).

The book edited by Aubrey (1994) is a collection of essays on the role of subject knowledge in early years education. Their direct usefulness to practitioners is quite variable.

There is no one work on curriculum theory and the early years that we wish to recommend, although Anning's (1991) book, *The First Years at School*, is well worth reading. The two most stimulating readings are unfortunately hard to get, being American. The NAEYC/NAECSSDE position paper is excellent and the book edited by Kagan and Zigler (1987) contains a number of thought-provoking papers.

THE ORGANIZATION
OF THE LEARNING
ENVIRONMENT

Order in chaos

'The fool sees not the same tree as the wise man sees' says William Blake. The interested observer and the early years specialist can stand in the same room and look at the same busy children but see very different things. The wise specialist will discern patterns and purposes, order and organization, experimentation and consolidation, whereas the interested observer will see simply busy, happy children operating close to the brink of chaos.

The fool is not stupid and chaos is often a possibility. Consequently, carefully prepared and thoughtfully sequenced opportunities for learning together, with well-worn routines and rituals, provide a structure which both prevents a slide into chaos and provides a sound framework for children's learning.

In this chapter, we shall examine how teachers set tasks for learners in early years settings. We discussed in Chapter 3 the kinds of tasks they set and their relationship to the processes of learning. We shall now look at the relationship between task-setting, classroom organization and the use of teacher time as a resource for learners. Assessment will thread its way through these discussions and will be examined with particular reference to the use of teacher time and the organization of learning. We are also aware of the extent to which educators in early years settings manage the work of other adults, and we conclude the chapter with a discussion of how support staff and parents may fit into the frameworks for the management of learning we have outlined.

But let us start with a more general survey of the busy interactive system that is an early years room. With a symbolic interactionist framework in mind, let us look at the messages that are relayed and consider what is important in the room. The questions that one asks are obvious.

What is valued, adults' work or children's work? Is children's work displayed beyond 'reading' distance or is it to be 'read' and discussed at child height or in the books compiled from children's work? Is there coherence in what is being highlighted through display? What are children learning from it? What are the gender, race and economic messages in the home area or the shop? How comfortable is the reading or quiet area? Will it attract the active boys? Is the painting and science area simply a place where the boys go to experiment and the girls to tidy up?

We can look again, this time mindful of the need to see the adult as the most valuable learning resource in the room. Do the children have easy access to the materials they need? Are they trained in putting things back in the right place? Are there easily available follow-up activities to occupy the quicker children? Where is the main adult positioned, at the side or mostly at the centre of the room? Are a large number of children working independently of adults? How much time does the teaching adult spend talking with children in groups of varying sizes? Does the teacher or other adults appear to have eyes in the back of their heads? All the questions we have just raised relate to organizational and environmental issues that are directly connected to teaching–learning interactions.

It appears to be more obvious in provision for the under-fives than in school settings that the learning environment is crucial, because for many educators of the under-fives the environment is where the curriculum is located. The complexity of the learning environment for the under-fives and the tight interrelationship between the formal and informal curricula of these early years settings is exemplified in the 'early childhood environment rating scale' (Harms and Clifford 1980). Here personal care routines, furnishings and display, language-reasoning experiences, fine and gross motor activities, creative activities, social development and adult needs are seen as major constituents in the environments established to support the learning of young children. An extract from the scale relating to personal care routines indicates what we mean by the environment being an element in the curriculum. On a rating scale of 1 to 7, it describes a highly rated meal or snack time in the following terms:

> Well balanced meals/snacks provided on a regular schedule. Staff member(s) sit with children and provide a pleasant social environment during meals and when possible at snacks. Small group size permits conversation. Time is planned as a learning experience including self-help skills, talking about children's interests, events of the day and aspects of food (colour and where foods come from).
> (Harms and Clifford 1980: 11)

A more obvious relationship between environment and learning can be seen in the allocation of specific areas in a room to specific areas in the curriculum. This can be seen in the use of carefully resourced learning 'bays' in nursery schools or in mathematics, science and language areas in infant classrooms. These physical settings for the beginnings of the acquisition of subject knowledge fit well with the ideas we discussed in the previous two chapters. Getting inside the discourse is made easier in infant schools when the discourse is clearly supported by carefully planned resourcing and related activities. Children can begin to engage with science as a discourse in its own right in these settings without it losing its relevance and fun.

The selection and structuring of learning opportunities form a major part of the work of under-fives specialists. Alongside this, their overt roles as interactive educators is, as we have already indicated, more carefully conversational than directly didactic and is extensively driven by the curricular selections already made and the darting curiosity of young children. Similar conclusions may, however, be drawn from the way teachers in the primary school sector spend their time. Campbell and Neill (1994), in their examination of primary teachers' time, have revealed that the teachers in their study spent on average 30 per cent of their time in preparation and assessment compared with 35 per cent of their time teaching in classrooms. Clearly, creating a learning context is also important to teachers of older children. Campbell and Neill's study showed that the practitioners they studied worked on average 53.5 hours a week. If that 30 per cent could have been reduced it would have been. It was the easiest set of activities to cut as it is the least visible area of teachers' work. What, then, makes it a worthwhile use of teachers' time?

We return to chaos and the pedagogical paradox outlined in Chapter 2. The tension between the selfish individual, the personal process of learning and the unselfish conformity required of groups of young children, if they are to exist as physically safe social groupings in which some individual learning can occur, is a challenge that is managed daily by early years practitioners. Young children with a limited concentration span and often enormous curiosity are not the easiest of groupings to control and organize. To manage them while directing their learning in ways which will enable them to operate effectively as they move through the education pathways available to them is not a haphazard activity.

Successful practitioners illuminate the pathways and keep the journey going at a pace that is neither breathless nor turgid. Illuminated pathways imply the curricular goals we have discussed in the previous two chapters. Learners who stray out of sight of these pathways can find themselves in tangles which can delay them and from which the teacher may not have time to extricate them with the necessary attention to what they might have learnt from the deviation. In order to attempt to keep learners on curricular pathways, teachers illuminate or highlight what is important. Doyle's work (Doyle 1986, is a useful summary) is particularly helpful in understanding how and why expert teachers do this.

His examination of classrooms and the coping strategies used by both teachers and learners allows us to see the enormous complexity of classroom life, the array of stimuli available to children and the confusing situation-specific behavioural rules. Later in this chapter we shall examine how teachers reduce cognitive confusion by highlighting the aspects of a task that require attention. At this point, we are considering the environment in which learning is occurring. Confused children waste adult time. Children who are able to interact independently with available resources in order to experiment, explore or consolidate, release adult time for teaching. Consequently, successful teachers reduce unnecessary complexity of the array of stimuli available, indicate clearly what is important and can provide a curricular justification of each display, resource or activity area.

Simplification and clarification do not mean that children are pushed towards activities with meaningless goals. On the contrary, the meanings become clearer as the mystification is reduced. Children's activities, as a consequence, are carried out less to please the teacher than to achieve a goal that can be seen and shared between teacher and learner. Mystification was one strategy that some early years teachers in the past used to enhance their control over children in the name of the 'magic' of the early years of school. While mystifying the learner sometimes made teacher control much easier than it might have been, the outcome for the learners was often bewilderment. Edwards and Mercer (1987) were kinder in their attributions for this practice than we have been and put it down to the fact that teachers felt that telling pupils things inhibited pursuit of 'their own individual potentials'. The outcome is, however, a similar bewilderment on the part of learners.

Once one decides to work with a subject structure of curriculum, mystification and bewilderment become inhibiting strategies. Expert knowledge in any subject is so complex that it has to be the result of a slow, carefully structured programme of induction into that subject knowledge. Key skills and concepts have to be identified and made clearly available to learners. Easy access to these key features of expert knowledge is part of the groundwork that early years teachers provide. This demands of early years practitioners both sound subject knowledge and a sophisticated understanding of how that might be translated into forms that will be understood and worked upon by young children.

Creating harmony

Teaching a lively interactive inservice session with experienced and informed practitioners is like a gig in a jazz club. Like expert jazz musicians, tutor and students work with a tune provided by the leader (tutor) who issues the challenge or demands a new angle as the playing becomes stale or dull. The lead is sometimes taken by the saxophonist or bass guitarist who will also challenge the leader, and everyone gives the apparently self-effacing drummer an opportunity for a solo. Everyone leaves the session exhilarated, stretched and with new insights into familiar themes.

Teaching young children, whatever charms it may hold, is not like that. Talking of older children, Doyle (1986) uses the image of the classroom as the circus ring in which the teacher is the ringmaster who ensures that the performers are all on task and working at the appropriate pace. Jones and Mercer (1993) talk of teacher as an orchestrator of the computer-based activities of children in classrooms. Doyle's image, with its focus on performance and control, captures important features, not the least of which is the difficult management role of the teacher. The second image, however, goes further in recognizing the amount of time spent by the orchestrator in arranging the score before the performance starts and the planning of the lulls, crescendos and the solo performances that occur in one teaching and learning session. The teacher as orchestrator knows the limits and potential of the instruments and players. Equally, she or he is aware of the conventions of the pieces to be played and the expectations of the audience. But even this image lets us down because the picture it presents is again one of final performance. Young children are not always ready for this. They need to explore the limits of their instruments, to recognize, learn and practise their scales, to acquire the ability to listen to others and enter on time. The early years environment is often in danger of resembling the cacophony of a set of practice rooms without sound-proofing. Young children are inexpert players who need to acquire the basic skills and become attuned to the sound expected in the different types of music they play and from the different instruments they use.

Teachers of young children, as we have already said, have a difficult job. They have to orchestrate the rehearsal more frequently than do teachers of older pupils. Teachers of expert adults can more easily join in the playing and learn themselves.

Doyle's observations of teachers and pupils again provide insights that can help us explore just how harmony is achieved in early years settings. His work is subtle and useful because it allows us to differentiate between the orderly classroom in which the *management of children* is the objective and the orderly classroom in which the *management of learning* is the desired outcome. In the former, order is achieved by keeping children on safe repetitive tasks which they can confidently achieve (skilled scale playing); in the latter, it is achieved through building on the basic skills to offer challenges and the opportunity to explore new instruments (unpredictable sounds) or to recontextualize existing skills and understanding (tune-playing).

Doyle's observations in classrooms suggest that in most classrooms neither children nor adults want chaos. The children usually want an easy life in which the teacher is satisfied and learners don't run the risk of failing publicly (see Chapter 2). Equally, teachers daren't risk public failure. Consequently, they need to ensure that they don't push the children to the extent that the learners will fear failure so much that they will refuse to cooperate. As a result, a series of negotiations occurs in classrooms. These are most obviously recognized among older children who will 'bid down' those challenging tasks which have been designed to assist recontextualization but which carry more risk of failure, into lower-level, more routine tasks. They do this by demanding more and more information from the teacher until much of the challenge is lost and a safer more routine task, based on teacher instructions, is substituted.

Younger children lack those negotiating skills but have their own ways of manipulating the carefully orchestrated plans of the teacher. Techniques range from reinterpretation of challenging tasks to similar more familiar ones (yet another Lego house appears), through rushing at the carefully prepared worksheet and using the space needed for the next activity, to timidly refusing to engage in the activity arranged in order to stand and watch. The hours spent by practitioners beforehand in orchestration are wasted and the temptation to keep to unchallenging activities is enormous.

We shall look at ways of providing opportunities for private failure and risky activities when we examine groupwork later in this chapter. At this point, we want to look in more detail at the processes of negotiation that are used by both teachers and learners and how they might be used to educational advantage.

Negotiation implies goals. Teacher goals are related to curriculum and class control. Learner goals are usually the maintenance of self-esteem (Chapter 2). As Doyle has pointed out, teaching and learning negotiations occur round the tasks that teachers set. Teachers set tasks to provide a sense of order or control; they also design them to provide an opportunity for children's learning. To plagiarize T.S. Eliot, teachers measure out their days in pupils' tasks. Tasks are therefore pivotal features of educational settings. Learners, however, can only react to tasks. They can do this in a variety of ways. They can endeavour to make sense of the tasks and complete them carefully, they can choose to misinterpret them and make them easier, they can simply misunderstand them, or they can ignore them. Ignoring them is difficult. It is a public transgression and punishable. Consequently, one of the remaining three options is usually taken. If teachers want tasks to be learning opportunities to enable learners to meet curricular goals, they therefore need to ensure that misinterpretation and thus misunderstanding are difficult to achieve.

Tasks need to be structured so that the type of outcome expected is clear and the stages involved in reaching that outcome are understood. Our examination of match in Chapter 3 indicates that we see tasks as often quite small-scale activities which support a longer-term cycle of learning.

Setting tasks

The conversations that occur when teachers set tasks for learners should have the following features if teacher orchestration or planning is not to be in vain.

◀ *Clarification of task goal*: for example, a plan for a home for the guinea-pig, through discussion and the examination of other plans the children have drawn.

◀ *Clarification of important features of the task*: for example, attention to the nutritional and environmental needs of the guinea-pig.

◀ *Diagnosis of what the learner already knows*, so that new information can be provided if necessary.

◀ *The opportunity for the learner to self-evaluate as the task proceeds and when it is completed*: for example, discuss and agree a list of basic guinea-pig requirements when the task is set.

When these features are coupled with resources that ensure rough drafting occurs, that final plans are drawn and that there is the opportunity to check and evaluate as the task proceeds, we have an activity on which it is difficult to negotiate or bid down to routine. It is also one in which language, supportive scaffolding and learner self-evaluation can find a place. Curricular goals are being met and learners are being stretched. What that task-setting process lacked was the opportunity for failure and bewilderment. This is clearly not a nursery school task. Younger children will need considerable help as they acquire the skills of self-evaluation.

Task design is a highly skilled activity. The guinea-pig task was carefully structured so that the learners were using or practising their plan drawing skills, which were already mastered, as a vehicle for considering the needs of animals. They were also developing their own ability to self-evaluate and justify their design decisions. Having planned the activity, the teacher needed to highlight the key learning outcomes of the environmental and nutritional needs of the animal and the self-evaluation skills of the learners. If children side-tracked themselves into, for example, designing armoured guinea-pig cages or pretty and cosy cages, they would first have bid down the activity and second have lost a carefully planned opportunity for developing their understanding of something they needed to know. One of the major outcomes of the introduction of the national curriculum has been the need to undertake quite detailed task analysis. In Chapter 3, we looked at different types of task demand and their place in the learning cycle. This included whether they were initial introduction tasks, tasks which involved some deeper restructuring of current understandings, or tasks which allowed practice in the use of newly acquired skills and understanding. In this chapter, we have added the need to consider the clarity of task goals and the important part that teachers play in highlighting what is important in a task if the opportunity for learning is to be maximized.

Since the national curriculum was implemented, task analysis has resulted in the need to justify tasks in terms of what children might *learn* rather than what they might *do*. It is a subtle difference but one that does place the *learning child* quite centrally in the concerns of the teacher. Tasks might still serve important control needs in classrooms by keeping children in order, but planning has become more explicitly related to children's learning. And whatever misgivings we might hold about the content, sequence and manageability of the national curriculum, the increased sophistication in task planning that it has achieved is, we think, to be welcomed.

The teacher as a resource

Although considerable teacher time was expended with the children in planning the guinea-pig task, the effects of the careful pre-session orchestration would have been lost had the teacher not spent so much time alongside the children clarifying goals and checking the existing scaffolding. Teacher time is clearly an important resource.

Our survey questions on the teacher as a resource at the beginning of this chapter were selected to reveal the extent to which the classroom was a self-running system. A teacher who acts as guardian of the store cupboard cannot be as available for scaffolding conversations as one who has carefully resourced that day's activities and trained the children in the management of those resources.

Similarly, the teacher who sets out his or her room so that teacher movement around the centre is difficult is forced into operating at the perimeters of the space available and at a distance from a number of the children. Those who place furniture at the edges and create a central space for themselves find the watchful monitoring and the quick scaffolding conversation much easier to achieve. As a resource, the centrally based adult is more conveniently placed for most of the children than one who cruises the periphery.

Conversations between teachers and learners serve different purposes at different stages in the cycle of learning we outlined in Chapter 3. In the early stages of the cycle, practitioner time alongside the learners is very important. Using the conversational interactional mode, the practitioner helps to shape the ways the children might make sense of a new experience. Appropriate and useful language is fed into the conversation by the adult and repeated regularly so that children become familiar with new words and their patterns and begin to attach them to the actions that are occurring. Once a child has started to make these connections, she or he can be moved into the second stage. Here teacher time is spent in watchful monitoring and shorter interventions to keep learners using the language appropriately. A child will be placed with others on a task that is resourced with the intention that the newly tried ideas and skills will be discussed and used. The third and final stage requires little teacher time, as here – assured that learners have some grasp of the ideas and skills – tasks are set up which enable them to practise and eventually to use understandings and skills in different contexts.

In most educational settings, these three stages are seen as initial whole-class or large-group interactions followed first by paired or small groupwork and then by individual or again small groupwork. A session plan that incorporates these three stages might look like that in Table 6.1. Key features of the plan shown in Table 6.1 include the following points:

◀ Desired learning outcomes or curricular goals are leading the task design.

Table 6.1 A teaching and learning session

Children	Learning outcomes	Task	Resources	Teacher time
Whole class		Allocation of tasks to yellow and green groups		(i) High
Red group	Practice of plan drawing together with development of self-evaluation skills	(i) Initial discussion (ii) Plan guinea-pig cage (iii) Evaluate	Previous plans by children Paper, pencils rulers, books on feeding animals	(i) High (ii) Medium (iii) Low
Blue group	Consolidation of understanding of needs of animals	(i) Initial discussion (ii) Plan guinea-pig cage (iii) Evaluate		(i) High (ii) Medium (iii) Low
Yellow group	Consolidation of understanding of features of animals Development of observational skills	(i) Close observational drawings of guinea-pig (ii) Individual reading with teacher	Guinea-pig, paper, pencils Reading books	(i) Low (ii) High
Green group	Exploration of features of wet sand and water Use of language to describe features and introduction to recording	(i) Sand and water (ii) Discussion of activities (iii) Drawing with some writing	Activity guide cards, toys, paper, pencils, crayons	(i) Low (ii) High (iii) Medium
Whole class		Evaluation		(i) High

◄ Attention is paid to resourcing in planning.
◄ Opportunities for independent learning activities are available for the purposes of both exploration and consolidation.
◄ Teacher time is allocated to children's tasks.
◄ Opportunities are made for pupil self-evaluation and risk-taking.

These are the structures and processes that the wise practitioner in our opening paragraph was able to discern. Both the orchestration and management of these have to take into account the following dimensions if the management of learning is to be the aim:

◄ curricular aims and demands;
◄ children's existing knowledge and skills;
◄ availability of practical resources and spaces;
◄ availability of teacher;
◄ current understandings of how children think and learn.

Managing learning through groupwork

We have already indicated in our discussion of teacher time that one strategy available to teachers is to think in terms of grouping children together and then to deploy their own valuable time in ways that suit the learning needs of groups. Let us now look at group work from another perspective and see how it might also be justified in its own right as a way of maximizing the ways in which children may best acquire curricular knowledge in inter-action with one another.

Teachers can use groupings in all three of the stages of learning we outlined in Chapter 3. They may select the large-group or whole-class groupings of the introduction and final evaluation activities, they may plan the paired or small-group activities engaged in by children as they try to make sense of and use newly introduced ideas and skills, or they may set up groups for undertaking problem-solving activities or some other kind of demonstration of understandings and skills. While grouping children in stages one and three (introduction and demonstration) makes the job of teaching much easier, grouping in stage two – the sense-making stage – serves an important educational function in its own right. We therefore focus our discussion on that stage.

In our examination of Doyle's studies earlier in this chapter, we sug-gested that the higher challenge tasks that require children to move beyond simple routine thought and action are often bid down into the more routine by learners who wish to avoid the risk of public failure and so maintain their own self-esteem. We now suggest that the management of both pupil esteem needs and the demands of curriculum content can be met through careful use of the safe, semi-public arena of teacher-monitored small learning groups.

These groups can be designed in a variety of forms. The work of

Bennett and Cass (1988) has demonstrated that the ways in which mixed-ability grouping in small groups is structured can have profound effects on the learning of the children involved. For example, if two high-ability children are grouped with one of low ability, the lower-ability child benefits little. However, if the grouping is revised so that two lower-ability children are grouped with one of higher ability, all the children learn. The higher-ability children they observed seemed to learn in any grouping, while homogeneous groupings of both medium- and low-ability children fared worst throughout the study.

These findings can be justified in Piagetian terms as the single more able child will need to clarify the disjunction between his or her understandings and those held by the others and so ease the accommodation processes required of the less able. They can also be explained using Vygotskian frameworks as the single more able group member mediates culturally held understandings and inducts the others into them in order that they can operate as a group. If teachers are to undertake such structured grouping, they need very detailed knowledge of pupils' understandings. The most expert of practitioners can be surprised by their own observations of children's language and performance in group activities.

Another less structured but equally useful use of groupwork is to see it simply as the opportunity for safe fumbling towards a competent use of concepts and skills associated with a subject area (Edwards, in press). This purpose demands tasks that require that learners talk while they act on the resources made available so that they can reinforce and mutually check understandings. It will also require careful teacher task-setting in which language use is emphasized and complemented by astute monitoring to ensure that the discussion remains on task. Here the centrally placed teacher uses the 'eyes at the back of the head' while talking with other children.

The kind of language that children use while working in these groping groups is important. Of course, the language which carries the key concepts – whether 'divide' or 'breathe' – needs to be essential to the task that is set. But in addition, even very young children can be taught strategies for group interactions which will stimulate their thinking. These can include remembering strategies: 'What happened when . . . ?' or 'Last time we . . . ?' They might involve questioning strategies: 'What if we . . . ?' 'How about trying . . .' They could involve listening strategies: 'What do you think . . . ?' They ought to at least involve an understanding of turn-taking and mutual respect if esteem needs are to be met. Phillips (1985), in a study with children aged nine to twelve, analysed the interactive group task of learners and identified strategies which are similar to those just outlined as those most likely to encourage pupil thinking. Once young children become competent challengers and thinkers able to work in groups, the teacher is liberated and able to undertake the important cultural mediation conversations that occur at the first stage of the cycle of learning.

We are not offering grouping children as a simple panacea. There is enough evidence available to suggest that simply placing children in groups will not enhance their learning. What we have attempted to outline are some of the conditions for effective groupwork. We are also aware that much of what we are saying about groupwork may be of much more relevance to the over-fives.

Independent learning

The work of Bennett and Dunne (1992) in collaboration with primary school teachers clearly indicates that well-run groupwork does free teachers from pupil dependency. The creation of an independent, self-managing learner is part of the groundwork that early years teachers undertake. But this kind of independent learner is not the socially isolated experimenter making his or her own meanings through acting on objects and events and creating through logical reasoning a construction of his or her world. In contrast, the learner we are describing is firmly embedded in a social world and accepts that tentative moves towards the mastery of the meanings shared by those deemed experts in that world are the necessary first steps to be taken, even by the most creative of thinkers. This kind of independent learner is learning how to access and process those meanings. In other words, she or he is learning how to learn.

An element in this form of independent learning is the ability to self-evaluate. We have already referred to the importance of self-evaluation in our discussion of children's identity construction and motivation in Chapter 2. We also indicated that it was an important feature of task-setting and task design earlier in this chapter. In Table 6.1 we suggested that the multi-focus teaching and learning session we had outlined should end with a whole-class evaluation period. Let us now pull together some of these ideas and examine their relevance for the organization of learning environments.

Self-evaluation can only occur if task goals are clear and we have already indicated that these are learning goals. There is, therefore, more to the form of self-evaluation that we are advocating than simple task completion. The tasks that are set are merely vehicles for the learning outcomes that teachers want to see learners achieve. Self-evaluation, therefore, has to incorporate an evaluation of what one has learnt, found easy and found difficult. This may be more easily termed as something one 'needs more tries at' or something one can now 'try to do in a different way'. Obviously young children will need help with this, but space for their own opinions to be heard in evaluatory conversations is an important step towards patterns of independent learning.

Group evaluation sessions are a useful forum for developing self-evaluation skills. In addition, they provide an in-built future checking device which will help to keep children on task. Importantly, they also allow the opportunity for children to demonstrate their mastery of concepts, skills and the associated discourse. Further, they are a chance for those who have already mastered the concepts and skills to revisit and revise them and for those yet to acquire them to have an initial introduction and familiarization with the language and ideas. Our own more recent observations in classrooms corroborate those of Kerry and Sands (1992). These suggest this kind of report back, evaluatory session is too often defeated by the need to complete tasks and tidy up. Evaluation is, it seems, sometimes regarded as a time-filling luxury rather than an essential element in the teaching and learning process.

Assessment in the learning environment

The pedagogic decisions made by teachers as they create the contexts we have been describing have all been led by a concern to guide and support children's learning and to deploy themselves as the most useful guide and support available. Assessment processes need to be incorporated into this view of teaching if they are to become part of the repertoire of early years practitioners. We are therefore not emphasizing summative assessments, but the daily formative assessments that drive the selection of tasks as practitioners plan their sessions.

Indeed, assessment is central to many of the decisions we have been describing. When children are moved on from tasks which give opportunities for tentative gropings to those which give a chance to demonstrate understanding, then an assessment has been made. The idea of the ZPD and the scaffolding constructed by teachers to support children through their learning zones is entirely dependent upon teacher decisions which are based on their assessments of what learners know and can do.

In this way, we can see continuous formative practitioner assessment as a form of cognitive map reading. If we link this view of assessment as a map reading of children's minds to our concern with the importance of adults as resources for learners, we can begin to create some criteria for useful assessment processes in learning environments. Criteria for useful forms of assessment are captured in the following questions:

◀ Do they provide information on which future learning tasks can be planned?
◀ Do they place more emphasis on assessment at the start of the cycle of learning than at the end?
◀ Do they involve listening to children as well as watching them and looking at their work?
◀ Do they recognize that teacher time should be spent on teaching; that assessment of mastery can be incorporated into the assessments on which teachers direct children through a ZPD; and that to assess for mastery when you know a child has achieved it is a waste of time?
◀ Do they recognize that mastery is an elusive notion and that young children in particular need to constantly revisit and revise?

Assessment that is undertaken to drive task planning and consequently children's learning should produce an affirmative to each of these questions. One of the most disappointing outcomes of the introduction of the national curriculum in England and Wales was the way in which assessment became conflated with reporting. As a result, assessment, recording and reporting became confused and assessment of pupils was in danger of becoming something for public reporting.

The assessment that drives teaching is, however, a private activity in which a teacher is as concerned to note what a child *cannot* do as what she or he *can* do, so that appropriate scaffolding can be built. Reporting on what the child can do, that is reporting of mastery, is relatively unimportant *if teaching and learning is our concern*. An emphasis on the mastery end of the cycle of teaching and learning diverts teacher time away from establishing the foundation of scaffolding required. And as any expert practitioner will affirm, mastery itself is pretty ephemeral in young children.

Our concern here is with assessment, how it is central to the management of learning issues we have been describing, and how it might be achieved with maximum benefit and minimum disruption and loss of time. Our premise is that it is impossible to run the kind of learning environment we have been describing without assessing children. The strategies we have outlined for assessing have included observation, listening, conversations with children and children's own attempts at evaluation of what they have done and learnt. When you add to these examination of children's writing or other forms of mark making, their artifact making, structured attempts at concept mapping and other more formal products, we can see that the additional burden on expert practitioners in recent years has not been assessment – there is nothing new in our list – but recording. Campbell and Neill (1994) found that the primary school teachers in their survey spent on average 2.7 hours a week assessing pupils while they were teaching and 7.1 hours marking and recording out of the classroom.

Assessment has always been a feature of the work of those practitioners who put children's learning at the centre of their planning. Our own work with teachers suggests that the national curriculum has led more teachers to this form of planning. But for both groups, the burden has been the recording stage and to this we turn.

As we write, five years after the introduction of the national curriculum and its assessment demands, we are all too aware that despite attempts made by local education authorities, individual schools and some commercial concerns, the recording of teacher assessments remains haphazard in many schools. This is, we think, because of an understandable resistance among teachers to what is perceived as a complex process which is not worth the time that might be spent on it. And they may be right. If current government urging towards whole-class teaching is successful, it may not matter that slower learning children like those in the Bennett and colleagues' (1984) study, which we cited in Chapter 3, never do have sufficient time to consolidate, practise and slowly acquire the basic building blocks of a good understanding of the curriculum to which they are entitled.

Children	Attainment Target Statements of Attainment						Comments
Name	date ⊗	✓					Found story planning easy see profile folder
Name	date ⊗	✓					
Name	⊘	✓					Needs practice with 'd' 'b'
Name	✓						

Key ✓ = introduction (stage one)
○ = making sense (stage two)
\ = appears to have grasped it (stage three)

Figure 6.1   A recording system

Clearly, we are not happy with such a prospect. We therefore conclude this section by briefly looking at minimal but effective ways of recording children's understandings and competences. Much of what we shall discuss is derived from the effective practice we have observed. Our emphasis is on the minimal and the effective.

If an assessment system is to drive the pedagogical decisions made by educators, it needs to be based on the model of teaching and learning that also drives those decisions. We have offered only one model of teaching and learning in this text. Consequently, we offer one model of recording the associated assessments. Minimal requirements for the system are learning outcomes for individual children and an indication of where each is in the three-stage teaching and learning cycle we have discussed. A *recording* system that is truly *assessing* a child's needs as well as achievements, as opposed to a simpler *reporting* system geared at reporting achievements, needs space for the recording of unexpected outcomes or concerns. Consequently, teacher records are often messy working documents which need to contain essentially private data from which reports may be drawn. The systems that we are happiest working with are simple; for example, a page of A4 for an attainment target or elements of a target (see Fig. 6.1).

Some recording schemes use the three-stage model we are advocating and suggest the use of coloured sections to achieve a 'traffic light' effect. A disadvantage of that method is that it does not allow for additional recording of 'making sense' activities. The number of circles evident against a name and a learning outcome will indicate the ease or difficulty experienced by the child at that stage in the learning cycle. The system shown in Fig. 6.1 also allows mastery to be dated and cross-referenced sometimes to material in a child's profile folder. We therefore also recommend that the record grid is supplemented by *some* examples of what the children can do in a profile folder which contains dated *examples* of children's products. And we stress examples, not everything needs to be kept. It is, however, crucial that these records are completed daily and lead task planning. The written records are not records of achievement, though the profiles can serve that purpose. The records we are describing are documents that are the basis for planning. If they are not, then they need to be rightly resisted as time-wasting burdens.

Educators of the under-fives do not have the same curriculum demands to juggle, but they do have curricula. They also find themselves in the role of educational consultant or leader in teams with other adults. Forms of record-keeping which follow the frameworks if not the content we've just outlined may be useful ways of communicating the purposes of the activities that are set for children and the particular roles that other adults might play as they support the learning of particular children on those activities.

Managing other adults

This topic warrants a volume in its own right. Early years educators find themselves responsible for the work of adults from a variety of professional and non-professional backgrounds who are working with them for a range of reasons, which may include the development of their own educational confidence and self-esteem or the provision of highly skilled specialist support to particular children. Lally (1991) feels that the management of other adults is one of the most challenging aspects of the nursery teacher's role.

These other adults are often categorized as non-teaching support. Campbell and Neill (1994) conclude that although the management of this support is an important part of the work of some teachers, it is an under-researched area. An analysis of the management of learning environments confirms just how difficult it is to work with the notion of other adults as *non-teaching* support. All the adults that help to constitute the environment in which young children are learning become resources for that learning. We are all familiar with how four- and five-year-olds refer to every adult they contact in school-type settings as 'my teacher'.

The work of the qualified teacher in these contexts extends, therefore, to the detailed management of available human resources (see Chapter 8). This will of course include sharing both the goals and processes of some learning activities with support staff and some of the other adults available. It may also involve putting strict limits on the kinds of activity they may undertake. It will certainly – parental support permitting – involve support staff and some other adults in the motivational and other socio-emotional concerns that relate to the children they will talk with.

The task-related curriculum is easier to manage than the hidden curriculum, as supporting adults can be given roles that involve practical help with the scaffolding necessary for task completion. This often includes monitoring colour mixing, assisting with cutting or working through planned activities in the wet sand or water tray. The more hidden curriculum is harder to manage, but it is here that non-teaching adults are often most effective in passing on values and expectations. Young children will chatter to the adult who remains still at a cleaning or sorting chore in ways that they cannot with the mobile monitoring teacher.

Throughout this chapter, we have emphasized the importance of clarification and goal-setting. The early years educator has the additional task of sharing these with support staff and other adults if they are to become seriously engaged in supporting the learning of children in environments which are orchestrated by early years specialists. Team planning and feedback sessions consequently appear to be essential features of a system in which other adults are brought into the learning environment. There are implications here for the payment of support staff who are often paid at hourly rates. It is clearly impossible to separate these important pedagogical concerns from wider issues that relate to both curriculum and organizational development. These we shall tackle in Chapters 8 and 9. In the next chapter, we shall examine links between home and school and attend to some of the questions that are raised by involving parents as non-teaching support in early years classrooms.

Points for reflection

1 This chapter brings to a close the section in the book where we have looked at the work of effective practitioners in educational settings which have clear boundaries, e.g. classrooms. At this point, can you compile a picture of an effective practitioner in a nursery or infant school setting? What are the features in his or her practice that you would want to see or hear?
2 Are there any elements in your own practice that you would like to work on and develop?

Further reading

Doyle's work on task-setting is most clearly set out in Wittrock (1986). But you need to give yourself a day in your local university library to work your way through the piece if you intend to read it there. Doyle (1983) is also a good introduction. Bennett and Dunne (1992) is an excellent account of the value of group-work and how teachers made it work. Lally (1991) and Hurst (1991) give very useful accounts of effective nursery school practice.

PARENTS AND PROFESSIONALS

Where the power lies

There are enormous and important differences in the relationships between home and school when we compare the statutory and non-statutory phases of early years provision. Once children are in school, teachers as key holders to publicly codified knowledge assume a powerful position *vis-à-vis* parents. Although, as we shall see, the parent as consumer can challenge that assumption. The under-fives field is, however, as complex as the purposes and forms of provision available. Some parents will find themselves powerless as their 'at-risk' children are given mandatory places in day-care centres which may or may not have overtly educational aims. Other parents may have more choice about their children's attendance but will be relatively powerless because of the counter-demands made by their own socio-economic, emotional and educational needs. Others will choose to use available provision as a service, which releases them for paid work or time to be spent on other interests or responsibilities. Others will be involved powerfully and actively as members of, for example, management committees.

Pugh (1987) provided a 'five-fold dimension' of parental involvement in preschool centres. The five major elements in her analysis are: non-participation, support, participation, partnership and control. Three of these elements have further sub-categories. For example, participation is subdivided into 'parents as helpers' and 'parents as learners'. These five elements will have different definitions attached to them when they are applied to infant school settings or to nursery classes. But they do provide a useful framework for an examination of possible forms of home–school relations in the early years of education. A comparison of statutory and non-statutory provision reveals that although parental control of statutory provision may have increased through the enhancement of the powers and responsibilities of governing bodies, it is unlikely to ever equate with the degree of parental control evident in a management committee of a preschool playgroup. Equally, non-participation is more likely to be an accepted feature of most parents' relationships with schools, while participation is likely to be a desired feature of nursery provision in, for example, family centres.

The major demarcation in the balance of power that exists between home and educational settings lies in the extent to which the professionals concerned are ultimately responsible for managing the institution. Power will lie with those who are responsible. What then determines the nature of the relationship between professionals and parents is the mission or aims of the institution. Parental involvement is, as a consequence, harnessed to institutional policy and is shaped by it.

Consequently, it is usually an over-simplification to see the importance of good relationships between professionals and parents simply in terms of creating a bridge for the child between home and school in order to ease the transition into school. Most early years specialists in both under-fives and over-fives educational settings see their work with adults as a long-term investment. Dividends are claimed by practitioners as children proceed through their later education with informed and trained supportive parents or caregivers. There is also the possibility of additional rewards as these parents or caregivers will work with younger family members. That so many early years practitioners give so much energy to work with parents suggests that there is a consensus that it is a valuable activity. Large-scale evaluation is unfortunately difficult because control and experimental groups are impossible to establish for sound comparisons between different types of involvement and non-involvement. For important ethical reasons, practitioners have to rely on their own observations and compile case studies of small-scale successes.

Because evaluation of the subtle long-term processes and aims of work with parents has to be complex and takes more time than can usually be paid for, it has been difficult to prove successfully that parental involvement programmes are beneficial. Nonetheless, Hannon (1989) argues that parental involvement, in the teaching of reading at least, is unstoppable. The function of evaluation is therefore to steer those engaged in the activity away from any possible pitfalls. Our own experience of evaluation in this field over an extensive period has identified some pitfalls. Some of these we will discuss in the sections that follow.

Most studies of parental involvement suggest that practitioners involve parents in the work that they do for educational reasons. Parents and caregivers are enrolled to support, in a variety of ways, the educational purposes of the educational institution. This may be a personally empowering experience for the parent or caregiver, but if the development of parents is an aim, it is desired with the educational needs of the child in mind. The prime source of power in most institutions therefore lies with the professional practitioners as decision makers. This assertion leads us to consider in more detail why practitioners make the decision to collaborate with those who also care for the children they teach.

Parental involvement and equality of opportunity

Any attempt at justifying strengthening the links between home and school raises the ideological questions which can more easily be avoided when one thinks simply about how to enhance children's learning. Once nurseries and schools are forced to look at their educational aims, so that they can share them with parents in their parental involvement programmes, the values that are inherent in the narrow entitled curriculum can become apparent. The elevation of one set of standards over another, whether it is standard English over dialect or academic performance over craft skills, gives an indication of what is narrowly regarded as a successful citizen. The hierarchy of standards that is implicit in any national curriculum is certain to mirror those of some social groups and not others. Parental involvement is often pursued under the banner of providing equality of learning opportunities for children. However, unless it is carefully managed, it can become a vehicle for undermining the value systems of some social groups through implicit criticism of what these groups hold dear, whether dialect or craft skills.

A view of educationally oriented parental involvement as a goal that is so worthy that it is beyond critique can prevent even the most reflective teachers from considering their own value positions and those embodied by the curriculum they are operating. We are suggesting that before parental involvement is tackled as a priority in early years educational provision, considerable soul-searching is essential. This examination should include a questioning of what is to be shared with parents and why it is to be shared. Questions about how should arise when the what and the why have been clarified. Later in this chapter, we shall argue that soul-searching and resulting policy decisions cannot be undertaken effectively unless all staff, both teaching and non-teaching, are involved.

Attempts at answering the why and the what questions in order to find a rationale for parental involvement or improved links with children's homes and their community may not always produce comfortable answers. Tizard *et al.* (1981) traced the origins of the interest in the early 1980s in parental involvement in nursery and infant schools. The major threads in their analysis were the relatively new understanding of social influences on child development and a simplified view of working-class environment as contexts that were deficient and less effective in the preparation of children for academic success. The two sets of beliefs combined in the 1970s to encourage a deficit model of working-class parenting which might be improved by increasing contact between home and school. This deficit model can still be heard in current discussions about home–school links in the early years. In the 1970s, it was informed by the wo (1971), Blank (1973) and Tough (1976), and the empha development of complex forms of language use and as a the intellectual functioning of children in the family.

Tizard's later work (Tizard and Hughes 1984), wh tailed analysis of girls' interactions at home and in preschool settings, snowed that the girls in the study received more cognitive challenge at home than at school. These findings led to a reassessment of the assumptions that the experiences of working-class children were richer in school-type settings than they were at home. Stereotypical notions of working-class life were at last damaged.

It could be said that the attempts of the 1970s at encouraging parental involvement because of perceived deficits in the home environment rested on a set of assumptions about the supremacy of middle-class attitudes and values. An unkinder argument would be the suggestion that early years practitioners as a group were struggling to be recognized as professionals and were therefore willing to take on parental involvement schemes, as these schemes in fact depended on the maintenance of a distance between the competent professional practitioner and the underperforming parent.

Professional distancing may also have occurred as a totally understandable reaction to the 1980s assumption that parents and practitioners might be equal partners in the education of young children. This assumption undermined the specialist and professional status of practitioners. Practitioner action research studies of parental involvement programmes consistently demonstrated that, in fact, even the most open-minded staff had cut-off points beyond which they would brook no collaboration with parents. While the most resistant staff used increased distance as their coping strategy, the assumption that parallel involvement necessarily decreases professional distance has not always been confirmed.

In the 1980s, the intellectual inadequacies of a 1970s deficit/compensatory education justification for parental involvement gave way to a rationale that appeared more optimistic and, as we have said, more clearly based on the notion of parents as partners in the education of their children. During this period, we observed programmes of parental involvement in home–school reading partnerships (Topping and Wolfendale 1985) and in mathematics schemes (Merttens and Vass 1990). Yet behind this curriculum aim, a deficit model of parents still lurked. Parents might be harnessed to curricular demands, but the training that they received in how to teach their children as a by-product of involvement was also considered an important feature and parental deficit was assumed. Parental diligence in the tasks set for them was monitored by the need for them to communicate, often in pleasant jokey letter formats, with teachers. Teachers' own evaluations of the success of curriculum partnership projects would depend extensively on parental participation rates and the assumption that parents were unwilling educators.

When we examine concerns that dominate in the 1990s, we can see

...at although a working-class deficit model in all its 1970s simplicity has been laid to rest; other forms of deficit, operating under the guise of difference, are currently apparent. Teachers who are responsible for the delivery of a national curriculum have little choice over the broad principles of involving parents from homes where, for example, English is the second language. Teachers pass onto parents school information, curriculum content and other key features of school and associated culture. This information-giving is a corollary to giving pupils access to an agreed curriculum. But unless difficult questions about cultural supremacy are addressed by staff groups, the ways in which these issues are passed on may resonate of colonization and ultimately lead to alienation rather than collaboration or cooperation.

These are difficult topics without easy answers, but we suggest that they need to be discussed among practitioners before they invest the considerable energy required by a programme of encouraging home–school links or enhanced parental involvement.

Typical parents?

Any examination of why a nursery or school might wish to undertake a programme of encouraging links with the families of the children they teach will have to take into account their potential collaborators. Parental expectations and needs will create the possibilities for teacher action.

Some parental expectations present few difficulties for practitioners. The non-participating parents who are also supportive rarely express any difficulties. The disaffected non-participants are a challenge and some may belong to the group we shall call 'needy parents', whom we discuss in some detail later. Participating parents, as Pugh (1987) has already indicated, may be learners or helpers: the helpers are often a godsend, the learners we will discuss as needy parents. Though we recognize that not all learners are needy and that helpers find that they too are learning and developing valuable confidence and skills which may contribute to their own personal or career development. Pugh's final categories of partnership and control can, as we have already indicated, present some problems for practitioners, the most recent manifestation of which is the parent as consumer. We shall therefore attend to needy parents and parents as consumers as examples of extreme sets of demands that might be made by parents on those nurseries and schools that decide to interact more openly with parents. These issues apply to a lesser degree to the voluntary sector, but some key features remain constant across settings.

Needy parents whose own economic, emotional and/or educational deficiencies potentially inhibit the educational support they might give their children can consume enormous amounts of teacher time. They can present problems that schools are unable to address and ultimately demand that schools begin to operate as referral agencies. They are not a responsibility that can simply be handed to the reception class teacher as part of his or her home–school liaison duties. These parents will move on through the school, and unless they continue to receive support the efforts of the reception class teacher may be wasted as parental disappointment sets in.

The management and support of these parents can be a full-time and exhausting job and carried more easily by a team than an individual. Nursery workers will be more used to multidisciplinary teams than education specialists. But an increasing number of the schools which are operating in the field are discovering the advantages of directly involving community workers and adult education specialists in their work with parents. An added advantage of this kind of cooperation is access to the funding which is available to these partners but not directly to schools, for example from local initiatives or adult education funding. Our own experience of evaluating work in this field over the past fifteen years would lead us to suggest that work with needy parents is not to be undertaken lightly and is certainly a route which has to have the commitment of the whole staff.

Needy parents can be seen as clients of caring professionals rather than as potential partners. Parents as consumers are a distinctly different client group but are equally unlikely to be seen as partners. They are a product of a categorization of social roles which encourages professionals in the caring professions to see clients as customers with associated rights. Interestingly Tizard *et al.*, writing in the early 1980s, note the growth of parent consumer groups in the 1960s, of which the Advisory Centre for Education (ACE) was one of the first, as an influence on the tendency to involve parents in the work of nurseries and infant schools. The challenges that these relatively small pressure groups made to the teaching profession formed part of a climate in which education itself became the subject of major national debate and a topic that could be publicly negotiated and discussed. This grass roots movement has, in some ways, been supported by legislation which has encouraged a consumer view of the Welfare State in general and of education provision in particular. This is evident in the publication of a *Parents' Charter* and the idea of 'customers' rights' in education.

In the 1990s, we find ourselves with a curriculum which is not negotiated, with indeed a relatively fixed menu for children. The role of parents of children after five as consumers is now not so much to negotiate that menu in public discussion, but to demand that it is delivered effectively. Their function is to remind practitioners, in the statutory sector at least, of their accountability. Vincent (1993) examined these contradictions and found what can be described as bounded consumerism in her exploration of parental participation in a city's education service through the work of a city Parents' Centre. Her analysis of the themes at work in the centre summarize the points we have been raising. She emphasizes the illusory nature of participation, the hidden agenda and the push away from partnership to individual consumer-based relations:

. . . firstly . . . apparent attempts to increase participation may well prove illusory in substance; secondly, that moves to introduce participating processes are often motivated by a wish to legitimate the more general action of the institution concerned; and finally . . . the dominant political ideology shuns the ethos of collective citizen participation, preferring instead an emphasis on the role of the individual consumer.

(Vincent 1993: 231)

The parent as consumer is a notion that may be premised in part at least on a view of teaching as a technical operation rather than a complex profession. It implies that market forces can shape education. Cooperative partnership with parents is unlikely if a purchaser–provider, parent-as-consumer model of education holds sway. In this context, closer cooperation with parents can degenerate into public relations exercises in which schools' images are packaged. Interestingly, Hughes *et al.* (1993), in their study of parental attitudes to school, found that the majority of parents did not see themselves as consumers who were able to make consumer choices and almost half were puzzled by the term. It seems that this definition has yet to direct the way that parents see themselves in relation to schools.

The parent as consumer is a different form of client from the parent as deficient educator. The former definition springs from a notion of client as customer, whereas the latter has its origins in education as a caring profession. Neither may provide a particularly useful premise for all forms of parental involvement in school. Consequently, in a climate in which parents are being encouraged to see themselves as consumers, nurseries and schools may find that a discussion of parental involvement might benefit from an analysis of parents as clients and the possible advantages that might be derived from moving towards closer partnership with them. Close partnership with a sharing of aims may prevent the final emergence of parent as consumer.

Ways and means

Our discussion of parental involvement has so far been cautionary. The intention has not been to deter but to encourage lengthy consideration of the purposes of involvement and some associated misapprehensions. We feel that this period of soul-searching is essential as a clear identification of the aims of a parental involvement will give direction to the extent and limits of the activities that will be undertaken. Early years practitioners cannot work miracles and most already find themselves under immense curricular pressure.

Figure 7.1 places forms of parental involvement on a continuum which runs from a view of parent as client to one of parent as partner. It also allows us to distinguish between activities that take place during the

Parent on the premises

Parents as clients	Use a room for own social or educational purposes	Attend concerts and information evenings	Run toy and book libraries and help with concerts	Regularly help on mundane tasks, e.g. cutting and cleaning paint pots	Regularly supervise children's activities, e.g. cutting and pasting	Regularly lead children's activities, e.g. baking, reading
Parents as partners			Help children to make things at home	Raise funds and make costumes	Help on school trips and with sports activities	Reinforce learning started with practitioners, e.g. listening to reading / Teach their children on structured schemes

Parent off the premises

Attend sports days and fund raising activities

Figure 7.1 Types of parental involvement

working day in the school or nursery and those that can be described as extramural and occurring either in homes or at other sites outside the main educational setting.

The categorization of ways of involving parents is useful because it forces us to consider a number of issues. First, it allows us to see that parental involvement is a developmental process. If the intention is to move parents into closer partnership, practitioners need to place the parents they are targeting on this continuum and consider what is possible. We would argue that it is overly ambitious to attempt to shift parents from being concert attenders to becoming teachers on structured home learning schemes without considerable bridge-building.

The developmental element of this continuum is not simple because it does not only depend on the growing skills and confidence of some parents. In some cases, it will depend on the willingness of teachers to blur the boundaries between the work of teachers and parents. There are problems here as we have already indicated in Chapter 6. Parents who work closely with children in educational settings then become adults whose work has to be managed by the practitioners who have ultimate responsibility for provision for their children. In addition, the need to defend professional status that we discussed earlier in this chapter can come into play and make partnership an unlikely option.

A large number of the activities shown in Fig. 7.1 represent work that parents do to improve the resources available to their children. These resources do not only include the library books or computers bought with Parent Teacher Association funds, but also teacher time which is released from the more mundane tasks that are all too essential to classroom management. This form of involvement is widely available and much appreciated but brings us back to the purposes of parental involvement.

Parents will not become better teachers of their children if they spend their time with other parents in their own work room repairing the spines on library books or cutting out crowns for the nativity play. But by undertaking these mundane tasks they release teacher time. They may be useful monitors of children as the children cut and stick jewels onto the crowns, but one has to query the educational purpose of such an activity without the presence of a trained practitioner able to exploit it for a discussion of colour, pattern and shape. It has to be at least questioned whether they have the ability to lead activities which might maximize the learning that can occur for a group of children, for example engaged in a baking activity, without training in group management, the conceptual structure of the subjects being covered and the language formats that might be reinforced. Loenen (1989) reported an evaluation of a school-based volunteer reading programme with junior school children and found considerable discrepancies between the approach recommended by the volunteers and their actual practice. This was particularly evident in the areas of reading for meaning and talking with the children. She concludes that more professional help for the volunteers might improve their effectiveness. Parents might be good educators of their own children at home, but despite the domestication of much early years provision, educational settings are different.

Our own work with practitioners has indicated that most parental involvement initiatives have not been premised on any analysis of the cycle of children's learning, or analysis of the types of tasks that are given to parents to undertake with their children, and the interrelationship of these two elements. One has to ask: 'Participation for what?' An analysis of children's learning and the role of the adult in it using the frameworks given in Chapter 3 might be somewhere to start.

Teachers are well aware of these issues. We have frequently observed the contradiction that schools justify their considerable efforts in the field of parental involvement in parental deficit and equal opportunities terms but operate systems which are geared at releasing teachers from mundane work. The decision to keep parents away from children may have been wisely taken given our concerns with the purpose and quality of conversations in learning environments, but may sit oddly with the espoused aims of the programme.

These concerns lead us to consider parents as partners in educational settings within a wider political framework. Underfunding of early years provision has led to the use of an untrained, unpaid, largely female workforce to sustain attempts at achieving what is described as good practice in early years provision. This has to be a topic that is at least discussed when schools undertake and evaluate their work with parents.

Other topics for discussion that arise from an examination of the purposes and processes of parental involvement include the role boundaries of practitioners and parents, the rights and responsibilities of each in the use of the premises and resources, and above all the educational purpose of each action that is undertaken. Practitioners take it as given that their actions have to be justified in relation to children's learning. It may be more difficult to keep parents to such a tight agenda. Once practitioners lose control of the agenda that determines the range and style of involvement, the aims and nature of the school or nursery may themselves shift. We have been warning throughout that although parental involvement may be a worthwhile venture, it is not without its risks.

Parental involvement and whole-school policies

We found in Chapter 2 Mead's notion of symbolic interaction to be helpful in understanding how children learn to categorize their social worlds and themselves within them. We also drew on this notion to begin to explain the distinctiveness of subjects and the need to get inside a subject so that one might operate with it. We shall now refer to symbolic interactionism in order to reinforce the claims we have been making for the importance of a whole-school policy if parental involvement programmes are to be effective in achieving their aims. The sharing of meanings between staff is an obvious first step.

Perhaps more than any other institutional policy, parental involvement requires that as many members of staff as possible are engaged from the first flickering of an idea. This will ensure that time can be given to soul-searching and careful examination of the purposes of involvement. During this period, the language used to justify involvement can be clarified and what is important to the school and its community can be made explicit. In addition, attention to the beliefs and feelings of staff at an early stage may mean that some of the contradictions we have discussed in this chapter can be avoided as differences are opened up and faced and meaning ultimately shared.

Once policy aims have been agreed, strategies can be selected. Our advice here is to be incremental and not over-ambitious in what you set out to achieve. Again the maximum involvement of staff is crucial and individual staff will have to feel comfortable with the actions they will undertake and be aware of their meanings and implications. If discomfort occurs, role boundaries will harden and professional resistance to involvement will result.

The selection of strategies needs to be followed up by in-house staff development during the period in which initial action is being prepared. This staff development needs to be related to the aims and strategies to be employed. In the best examples training involves domestic staff and non-teaching assistants. If parents are to be encouraged to fulfil the roles available to them in the involvement scheme, the messages they receive from all the adults in the educational setting must be consistent. Here an understanding of symbolic interactionism helps us to see the importance of a consistent and coherent behaviour of all staff towards parents or caregivers. As staff chat to parents when they collect children or telephone with a query, a sense of parental rights and responsibilities within the school is conveyed and a set of expectations of parent as client or as partner is established in the language used and the tone of the interactions.

The extent to which parents themselves might be involved in the development of policy and selection of strategies needs to be considered. Yet again this is not an easy issue. We have argued already that the typical parent does not exist. One or two parents at the policy-making stage may exert unwarranted influence. It may, however, be possible to check the policy with existing groups of parents associated with the school. It would certainly be expected that the governing body might have a view on this policy. As strategies will stem from policies and be limited by resourcing and staff readiness for involvement, the role of any existing parental group might be as limited as to receive information and comment if it wishes to.

The development of policy and selection of strategies might usefully be informed by other professionals involved in work with local families. We have sometimes observed overlap between the activities of home–school liaison teachers and community workers. We have already indicated that other professional groups might have access to other strategies and additional funding. They may also offer insights into work with families that cannot be found in the training that education specialists receive. They will certainly alert education practitioners to additional pitfalls to be avoided.

Funding is another important reason why parental involvement needs to be taken seriously, as a matter that affects the whole school or nursery. Parental involvement activities can be expensive. This is particularly the case if home visits are involved or if staff time is spent in supporting parents as they prepare to work at home with their children. Decision making about funding staff to work with parents is yet another reason to put parental involvement programmes at the centre of school management concerns.

The open learning environment

We have so far discussed links between professionals and parents largely in terms of parental involvement initiatives. Yet many of the types of parental involvement shown in Fig. 7.1 are common occurrences in schools and nurseries which would not regard themselves as overtly operating a parental involvement policy. A common quality in these environments is an openness to others which is clearly evident to any symbolic interactionist. Children tend to move freely to and from main resource or teaching bases; a visiting adult causes no disruption; and the curriculum is enriched not only by constant interplay with the immediate nursery or school environment, but also by bringing the wider world into the learning situation, whether it be through a bunch of bud-laden twigs or a visit by a local firefighter.

Open institutions create situations in which a relaxed dialogue with parents can take place. This is imperative if discipline issues are to be tackled before they develop, if children with both major and minor special needs are to be accommodated, and if parents and practitioners are to share their understandings of what motivates or deters the children.

Openness of this kind implies a respect for parents as informed carers with a part to play in the education of their children. One problem with overt parental involvement initiatives identified by Brown (1993) is that they tend to establish models of ideal parenting against which parents are judged and usually found wanting. Public scrutiny – for the first time in some cases – of the products of their child-rearing can be stressful. To add to this a direct assessment of themselves as participating parents can be unnerving. A relaxed climate of mutual respect which is consciously supported by all members of staff may be the context in which the most useful and meaningful of conversations between practitioners and parents may occur.

Creating a climate for dialogue is not easy as both practitioner and parental attitudes can prevent this. Hannon and James (1990), in their exploration of parents' and teachers' perspectives on the development of preschool literacy, observed that only five of the forty highly concerned parents they studied actually talked to nursery staff about how they might work with their children at home. This was despite the majority belief that nursery teachers would be able to help them. Twenty-two of the forty parents felt that nursery education did help in the acquisition of literacy but were vague about how. Hannon and James also accuse nursery staff of vagueness. Interestingly, they comment that: 'In order for nursery teachers to communicate effectively with parents they need to be sure of what constitutes the nursery curriculum' (Hannon and James 1990: 269).

As we have already argued in Chapter 6, an open learning context depends on clarity of purposes and strategies if chaos is not to ensue. The school or nursery that can afford to take the risks involved in being open and maintaining permeable boundaries with the local community is usually the establishment where goals are clear, relate to children's learning and can be made explicit whenever necessary. In this way, spontaneity can be checked against children's learning needs and the best of both the worlds of home and school can be seen in action.

Points for reflection

1 Think of a school or nursery you know well. How would you describe the parents and their expectations of the school? Are they a homogeneous group of parents? How might the school best involve them if the school's aim is to enhance the learning of children?
2 Think of something you are aiming to teach a group of children. How might parental involvement support the work you are trying to undertake? How much help would the parents need to play their part well?
3 Do you see any conflict of values between your school's aims and those of the parents of the children at the school?

Further reading

Merttens and Vass (1993) is an interesting collection of papers. It focuses on a mathematics initiative but raises a set of issues which clearly need to be addressed if schools are to acknowledge the wide-ranging implications of working closely with parents. The National Children's Bureau publications provide some useful and accessible case studies of parental involvement at the preschool phase, though these collections lack the critique provided by, for example, Merttens and Vass.

DEVELOPING THE CURRICULUM

In Chapters 1 and 2, we outlined a vision of effective early years education. Among other things, we agreed that it is related to skill in interpersonal relationships, to patience, to having a good store of activities to hand, to diligence, love and care. However desirable such qualities are, they do not define effective early years education. That depends on two further areas of expertise. On the one hand, practitioners need to be guided by understandings of children, both as learners and as social beings who are mastering new contexts, new conventions. They need to be alert to children's self-esteem, and sense of efficacy; to the variety of teaching roles, actions and to the underlying knowledge bases; and they need to be skilled at task planning and assessment. Skilful development of learning environments and alertness to the complexities of learning are also called for. Yet learning is not an empty concept. Therefore, on the other hand, we need a view of *what* children learn, which in turn implies a view of *how* they learn. We have argued that the scope of early years education might be broader and more purposeful than has sometimes been acknowledged; and that the national curriculum offers no bad framework for curriculum planning, always given that the job is not to force content upon children in ways that destroy existing notions of good ways of working with young children. The job is to make the curriculum accessible to children and, by making it real and relevant, to blur the false distinction between child-centredness and curriculum-centredness.

Taken together, these claims amount to a definition of early years education. We have replaced some common but limited beliefs about good practice by arguing that they are essentially inadequate: fine as far as they go, but that they don't go nearly far enough. One consequence of our stance is that early years professionals are faced with a substantial job of curriculum development (this chapter) and organizational thinking (next chapter). We know that practitioners are already facing these challenges. The national curriculum is affecting years 1 and 2 and its backwash laps into the reception year. At the other end, there is parents' well-documented concern about what their children are learning in preschool provision. This is especially the case among what some American commentators have called 'cannibal parents' – parents who press so hard for their children to do too much, too formally and too early that they eat up their children's childhood. Third, there is government scepticism about the need for professional early years teachers, evinced in the recent suggestion that non-graduates might take on teaching work. That proposal may have been laid to rest but, Dracula-like, we suspect it will revive. In any case, it would be prudent to recognize that early years educators have not yet made sufficiently clear their claim to be professionals, and addressed the task of developing that case. We think that an urgent priority is to develop a view of professional activity that is suited to the next century (Taylor 1994), rather than harking back to the circumstances earlier in this century. We shall argue that this would involve practitioners in stressing their role as people making daily sense through their practice of complex knowledge about developing children, teaching, learning and the curriculum.

With this context in mind, we turn to the mechanics of curriculum development. Although this is located within our vision of early years education, what we have to say is relevant to early years curriculum development (and organizational development, in the next chapter) irrespective of the values and goals that practitioners cherish.

A technocratic approach to curriculum development

Sometimes, curriculum development is seen as practitioners acquiring new technical mastery. This form of curriculum development, which is an important one, focuses on practitioners learning more about techniques for teaching given subject matter. Reading non-statutory guidance for the national curriculum, books on teaching different curriculum components, attending information-giving and skill-enhancing inservice courses, and collecting ideas from colleagues and *Junior Education* all have value here. Without this knowledge-enhancing part of curriculum development, people are not able to develop curriculum but only to recycle existing (mis)conceptions, (good) practices and (limited) knowledge. Their scope for professional action is limited.

This type of curriculum development amounts to learning how to do new things that have been developed by others. We suggest the introduction of history to the national curriculum as an example of this. This was a new subject in many schools, a subject that was conceived of in new ways in other schools, and a subject that was to get much more priority in others. In all three cases, teachers had to master government prescriptions in the forms of programmes of study and attainment targets. Their priorities were to understand and to collect ideas for activities that would comply with the new demands. In many cases, a new understanding of history had to be built up. In others, it was a matter of adding new techniques or goals to existing activities. The common feature in each case is knowledge acquisition. Practitioners had to acquire a technical knowledge akin to a car mechanic who is to service a new model of car – a knowledge of what to do, a repertoire of activities.

This view of curriculum development depicts curriculum as a product to be delivered in bulk to teachers, who portion it out and deliver it in smaller packages to children. In a sense, there is value in this view of curriculum developed centrally and implemented locally. Teachers do need to know what the innovation amounts to and they do need to convey that to the children. Yet this view is essentially inadequate. Curriculum is not, and cannot be, a shrink-wrapped package: it is a set of ideas, principles and suggestions that are to be implemented, or vivified in classroom practice. What was planned is never what you get, since the act of creating the plans in practice changes them. Consequently, teachers are not postal workers but artists working in the medium of learners and learning. For the same reason, we ought not to talk of *delivering* the curriculum, since there is no package to deliver: there are sketches to be painted, over-painted and re-painted. Curriculum is an act of creation, not a product – or, as Hargreaves (1994: ix) put it, 'teachers don't merely deliver the curriculum. They develop, define it and re-interpret it too'.

Two analogies may help. Consider the case of Dr Frankenstein's monster. He assembled enough parts to make the monster, but simply arranging the parts was not sufficient to give it life, any more than simply collecting together classroom activities makes a history curriculum. What was needed was to energize the parts, just as the activities need to be infused with an understanding and purpose. Moreover, once vivified, Frankenstein's monster turned out to have what are now called 'emergent properties': it was not simply a collection of bits, but a being that was greater than the sum of the parts and which had a force of its own. So, too, with curriculum. What develops when the parts are bought together and invigorated is often unpredictable and problematic, but also special and valuable. The heart of professionalism is informed management of this process.

Or consider a Renaissance painter. Sketches based on close observation of life formed the basis of a painting but those sketches, while delimiting the finished product, did not define it. Not only does the different medium of paint bring textures and tones into the picture, producing something very different from the sketches, but as the painter painted, changes were improvised, sometimes substantial changes – characters were added, moved or deleted. Nor was it uncommon for the artist to change his [*sic*] mind and overpaint sections and produce, on second attempt, something quite different from the first, itself different from the sketches. If the sketches are like curriculum plans, we can use the analogy to show how practice, like painting, changes and usually enriches them.

Yet if it is grossly misleading to see curriculum as delivery, that should not make us forget that practitioners do need to do the educational equivalent of sketching or assembling the parts. There is no substitute for curriculum as technology, to the degree that teachers need to know, understand and be able to do history as a school subject. Always given that there is more to curriculum development than that, it remains important for practitioners to know curriculum as technology.

Therefore, we do not entirely reject a traditional, formal type of curriculum development which may, regrettably, assume that curriculum is something to be delivered. If it enhances knowledge, if it builds technical competence and awareness, if it makes teachers more like mechanics who can service a hundred models of car, then it is valuable. But valuable only as a precondition for proper curriculum development, as the equivalent of Frankenstein's collection from the charnel house, or of a painter's preparatory sketches. We are saying that criticism of this technical approach to curriculum development is exaggerated. It could also recoil on the teaching profession. A characteristic of any occupation that is accepted as a profession is that its practitioners are seen as people with access to a specialized body of knowledge (in this case, about children, teaching, learning and the curriculum) that has to be translated intelligently through practice. If teachers don't themselves accept that deep knowledge is a part of their work, they can hardly complain if others don't see teaching as a profession.

Figure 8.1 shows how additional knowledge may extend teachers' repertoires (top), without shifting their level of thinking (bottom). The spiral shows how this thinking has developed in the past but has now reached a balance that is not disturbed by curriculum innovation. The new knowledge is simply assimilated to the existing levels of professional thinking.

So one form of curriculum development is the acquisition of the new, key features of subjects that constitute the curriculum. A clear grasp of the key ideas and ways of knowing in a subject are, of course, crucial if task-setting and pupil assessment are to be carried out effectively, as we have argued in earlier chapters.

Curriculum development as action research

The second view of curriculum development rests on three premises: that the teacher is at its heart; that teacher development and learning are the key to development; and that all development takes place within the setting of special and complex circumstances which make each curriculum development distinctive. In the words of McKernan (1991: 253), 'curriculum will be improved by researching our own teaching'. Equally, 'the development of curriculum programmes occurs through the reflective practice of teaching'

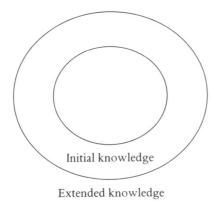

Initial knowledge

Extended knowledge

A stopped spiral
of development

Figure 8.1 Extension of knowledge without a development of professional thinking

(Elliott 1991: 54). This view has been variously labelled action research, classroom enquiry or reflective practice. These labels can be confusing. As we indicated in Chapter 1, we assume that all effective teachers are reflective teachers and modify their teaching on the basis of reflection *in* practice and reflection *on* practice as soon as possible after the event. The more systematic classroom enquiry that we call action research adds rigour to the essential review–plan–act–review cycle of effective teaching. Action research involves careful monitoring, the collection of evidence for further reflection and, above all, the testing of theory through practice. In action research, issues that arise in practice lead practitioners to further exploration in the research literature or to sharing and building theory with colleagues, and to the testing of these ideas in systematic ways in their own teaching.

It must be understood that most practitioner learning and development may be regarded as curriculum development, given that we have defined curriculum broadly, encompassing both content to be communicated and the ways of working implicated in doing so (Chapters 2–4). If we also include the 'hidden curriculum', then we might see that learning more about playtimes, revising rules and routines, and working with parents might also be seen as curriculum development. There is a maxim, attributed to the late Lawrence Stenhouse, that there is no curriculum development without teacher development. The reverse also has a lot to commend it.

Action research as systematic enquiry

We define research as systematic enquiry made public, again following Lawrence Stenhouse. An advantage of this definition is that it does not prescribe any particular method of study, freeing practitioners and researchers from the need to engage with natural science-like, quantitative research methods. Valid research methods are those which are fit for the purpose, rather than ones which are hallowed by various traditions. Therefore, it may be appropriate not to try and control the many variables at work in the class, to forget about testing for statistical significance and to accept that subjective impressions can be valuable as research data, as long as it is not forgotten that they are exactly that, subjective impressions. Small-scale studies, where data tell us about *this* class in *this* school at *this* time, are not only permissible, but they are also normal in action research. It is not the intention to generalize from individual action research to studies of classes and schools *at large*. The main beneficiary is the individual or group of practitioners who have gained food for thought or, to put it more grandly, hypotheses for action. Since the intention is to help the practitioner to reason better, these limitations do not undermine the concept of fitness for purpose.

Useful accounts of action research techniques are contained in Hopkins (1993), Hitchcock and Hughes (1989), Elliott (1991), McKernan (1991) and Edwards and Talbot (1994). One feature is sufficiently distinctive to need comment here. The problem with individuals researching their own practices is that they tend to see what they expect to see. The problem for them is making their own, taken-for-granted, eminently sensible practices problematic and open to analysis. Having another person observe them, while keeping a record of what happens, allows another perspective to be taken on the data. It allows one person's subjectivity to be set against another person's different subjectivity, both referring to a record of what happened. A second perspective, then, not only guards against capricious use of data, but it also makes for a dialogue about significance and meaning. However, it is often impossible to arrange this in busy classrooms. If this is the case, classroom data can still be collected and the data themselves become the focus of analytical discussion with colleagues. We would argue that the analytical conversations about the data are the most important learning element of action research for teachers.

If many techniques are acceptable within action research, we need to emphasize that the enquiries need to be systematic and that they need to be made public. By 'systematic', we mean that practitioners need to have a view of the problem that they are trying to unpick and to reflect continually upon connections and explanations as the result of data that are purposefully and appropriately collected.

The need to make the enquiries public points to the importance of research being in some sense a collective activity. Suppose that we have a hunch that younger children in a group are being rather ignored because the older children, more vocal and confident, make more pressing demands upon us. One way of investigating this would be to tape or video some sessions and count our interactions with children. Making this public could involve us asking colleagues for suggestions about which sessions to tape, where to place the recording equipment (often we cannot tape the whole group), how to tally the interactions (what do we define as an interaction?) and what to make of the results (is it perhaps older boys who make more demands upon us, rather than just older children?). Moreover, as we shall show, action research embodies a commitment to using the data to change the situation. Making the research public brings colleagues into thinking about how we might try to make a difference to it – and in helping us to decide whether our actions have made much of a difference.

Desforges *et al.* (1986) have gone further and argued that writing down one's reflections on practice is essential, since it is a powerful form of thinking. While we recognize that writing is a good discipline and a way of sharing findings with colleagues, we also recognize that some practitioners are reluctant to write, often saying that they have insufficient time to do so.

So action research is work on a human scale that involves us in sharing our thinking with colleagues. Six other features are:

Practitioner learning is at the heart

Nias and her colleagues (1992) found that schools undertaking whole-school curriculum development were committed to professional learning. This curriculum development went ahead in ways that could be described as action research. Rosenholtz (1991) said that teachers in effective schools emphasized that their own learning was central to their job. This learning had much in common with action research. Not surprisingly, she described the schools in which this attitude predominated as 'learning schools'. Action research may be seen as teachers learning directly but systematically from their own experience. In contrast, they may learn nothing from engagement in other forms of research, or indeed, from daily practice. As Fig. 8.1 suggested, just knowing more about ways of teaching might be no more powerful. This latter point is worth developing, since it shows that action research is not the same as any form of thinking about learning and teaching. To develop this point, we need to draw upon a simple model of teacher thinking (see Fig. 8.2).

While it is clear that planning and thinking involve the interplay of values and beliefs, practice, and evaluation, this model is essentially circular. Beliefs need not be affected by our daily thinking and practices. Indeed, our beliefs can lead us to perceive and interpret our practices in ways that cause no upset to either, with the result that evaluation and reflection merely confirm the self-reinforcing circle.

An example of this is the practitioner who believes that children's

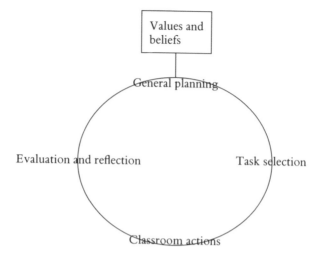

Figure 8.2   A model of teachers' thinking

failings are ascribable to faults in themselves, their homes or backgrounds. Often such practitioners still manage to credit themselves with children's achievements. Faced with children whose behaviour is unacceptable, or whose speech is faltering, such practitioners are, first, not likely to wonder whether there is anything in the educational setting that might have a bearing on these phenomena; second, they will not make changes in an attempt to make a difference; and third, their exasperation with the state of affairs is likely to reinforce their beliefs, not to call them into question (see Fig. 8.3).

Being reflective, in the sense of just thinking about the job, is not enough. We need to be *critically* reflective, which is to say that there need to be ways in which our beliefs, assumptions and practices can be jolted. Rosenholtz characterized this commitment to exploration as something that marked out teachers in 'learning schools'.

Action research, because it involves systematic data collection and dialogue with colleagues, offers a way of producing learning, in the sense of professional development, rather than thinking that reinforces established cycles of self-confirming reflection.

Practitioner ownership

Much formal research is carried out by people from outside the classroom who take practitioners and their children as the subject of research into problems identified by, and of interest to, the researchers. Once the research is done, it and the conclusions are the 'property' of the research team, which then tries to disseminate it to practitioners at large. Inevitably, their findings will be couched in generalizations and be short of sensitivity

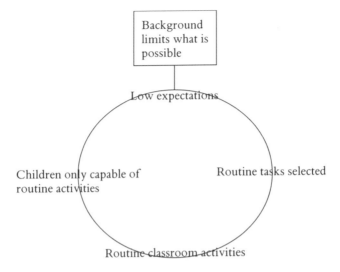

Figure 8.3 Beliefs as a constraint on practice

to the critical conditions and variables that make each educational setting special. Such findings may also be presented in terms that are unfamiliar to practitioners, which they see as jargon.

Action research often starts with a practitioner's unease with an aspect of her or his practice. The research is done by the practitioner to be useful in relation to the setting in which she or he works. The findings are the practitioner's and do not need to be disseminated, nor to be translated or interpreted further than the educational context in which they originated. The practitioner owns the research – its definition, methods, context and meanings. There is no researcher–practitioner gap, since researcher and practitioner are one and the same.

An important aspect of this issue of ownership is that the practitioner's values underpin and guide the research and are clarified through it.

Action research is about making a difference

The value of action research lies largely in its emphasis on action. Action research is not study for the sake of curiosity, although it often has its beginnings in curiosity. It is research that leads to action which is evaluated, and often re-researched and re-refined. In Elliott's (1991: 49) words, 'the fundamental aim of action research is to improve practice rather than to produce knowledge', and he defines action research as 'the study of a social situation with a view to improving the quality of action within it' (p. 69).

It ought to be seen as a spiral in which each action is based upon systematic enquiry and which, on inspection, turns out to have produced a change that needs to be refined and evaluated in turn. It is like the mathematical procedure of successive approximations, where several attempts are made to get from a crude answer to a better one. Or, to quote Hargreaves (1994: 138) again: 'reform is often guided by the belief that every problem has a solution. Perhaps the real challenge of reform as a continuous process, though, is acknowledging that every solution has a problem'. Action research, professional development and school-based curriculum development are all continuous processes. Other research is not so directly tied to making a difference and simple, self-confirming reflection may actually inhibit change. The touchstone of action research is that practitioners use research to influence action. And again and again.

It is flexible

Outside researchers are often locked into a set of methods and to a research timetable. Action researchers have the freedom to work at a pace that is comfortable, that recognizes that some times of the year give more scope for research than do others, that some times of day are easier than others and that some sessions may be more revealing than others. Where outside researchers are often looking for sessions that are so typical that they are almost untypical, action researchers can alight upon particularly revealing sessions at their convenience.

Action research is collegial

Because action research is often, though not always, enquiry made public within a school, it ought to influence colleagues. It might involve them directly as collaborators, or it might provoke them to readdress their own ideas. This is desirable on three counts. First, a profession is, among other things, a body of practitioners who talk to each other, sharing ideas, problems and practices. Second, there is a view that teachers' pervasive professional isolation is pathological and that teaching – perhaps teachers too – could be improved by more collaborative patterns of working. Third, many commentators believe that school improvement comes through whole-school action, in which collaboration and collegiality are necessary.

Some caution is needed in the face of this celebration of collegiality. Hargreaves (1994) has argued that there are sound reasons for teacher individuality, and that much that passes as collaborative work is, in fact, contrived and wasteful of teachers' energies, contributing to the intensification of their work, while other collaborative work is low-level and short-term in nature. 'Teacher empowerment, critical reflection or commitment to continuing improvement are claims that are commonly made for collaboration and collegiality in general, but in practice they apply only to specific versions of it' (Hargreaves 1994: 188). Elliott (1991) has expressed related fears, that action research may be used in a technocratic fashion, as a way of getting teachers to investigate and concentrate upon the technical issues of curriculum delivery [sic], distracting them from questioning the values that underpin the curriculum prescriptions that they are trying to deliver.

Yet the collaborative potential of action research *is* a bonus, always assuming that practitioners are alert to the way that action research, like professional commitment, professional development and the professional ethic of care, can be turned against them. It is also possible for the practitioner to work alone on action research.

Action research is professional activity

McKernan (1991: 48) claims that 'research activity is a *sine qua non* of the professional'. This rather depends upon how you define 'action research' and 'professional'. If by 'action research' we have in mind something that is pregnant with the possibility of changing practitioners' thinking and that is systematic, rather than simply normal classroom thinking, then action research is important to professionals. These professionals are people who are regularly engaged in checking their espoused theories (which embody the propositions and principles of the profession) against their practices and its theories-in-use. Not all professionals do that, functioning instead as unreflective practitioners. And for the solicitor who is mainly engaged in property conveyance work, that may be quite appropriate.

In our view, the prime, distinctive feature of a profession is that it is, to use a Tudor phrase, a mystery: it has a body of knowledge that only the professionals can translate and apply. Those professionals are skilled in the application of these general ideas to specific situations, and become more skilled by purposefully contemplating their own interplay between theories and practices. In that view of professionalism, action research is necessary. Without it, professional growth is skewed and stunted, like a wind-blasted tree.

Action research and curriculum development

Action research is an eclectic process of public, systematic enquiry, ideally collegial in tendency, that is directed to making a difference to children's experiences of schooling. But how is this related to curriculum development?

In one sense, it isn't, since action research is not the main source of knowledge about the different subjects and topics that might be presented to early years children, nor is it the source of teachers' repertoires of techniques, nor of their initial values. It builds upon, and has the power to change, all of these. This amounts to a two-stage model of teacher and curriculum development. The first stage is the acquisition, by whatever means, of essential competences or knowledge (Aspland and Brown 1993). Apostles of action research are often quiet about this foundation work of becoming knowledgeable, of acquiring the technological knowledge of curriculum and schooling. Without it, practitioners' ranges of possibilities are constrained, and there is a danger that development becomes Procrustean development. In mythology, the bandit Procrustes had a bed which he claimed fitted any 'guest', be they short (in which case they were stretched on the rack until they fitted the bed) or tall (in which case they were trimmed to size). The main danger of curriculum development and action research is that innovation may be fitted into the Procrustean bed of existing, unchallenged assumptions about children, their homes, teaching and learning. One way of lessening that possibility is insisting that practitioners need to have as wide a range as possible of propositional knowledge – of ideas – about children, curriculum content, learning and teaching methods, and about education. It follows, then, that a school needs to ensure that formal curriculum and educational expertise is acquired and available.

However, action research is powerful in curriculum implementation, in assessing outcomes and in raising wider possibilities.

Models of action research

Action research is seen as a spiral of learning, with stages of enquiry (which do rather overlap each other) recurring at developing levels of understanding, sophistication and complexity. There are various, rather similar accounts of this, so we present just two as illustrations of the principles.

Whitehead (cited in McNiff 1993) proposed five stages:

1 Experiencing a problem in which my values are denied in my practice
2 Imagining a solution
3 Acting to advance that solution
4 Evaluating the actions
5 Modifying my ideas and practices.

Alternatively, McKernan (1991: 224) has described the first cycle of an enquiry as:

1 Define the problem (use a diary and video record in conjunction with discussion with colleagues to help this)
2 Work towards hypotheses and a plan of action, based on assessing the situation (use similar methods and write reports and memos)
3 Implement plan (collect data as above and discuss its meanings with colleagues)
4 Evaluate the plan as it's working out (collect data as above, but also use others to observe what's happening: identify key, emerging issues)
5 Re-plan (involve colleagues in this)
6 Implement revised plan (as 1, above)
7 Write a case study to present to colleagues
8 Go on to the next cycle.

Curriculum implementation and a history topic

Suppose that history is being introduced to the early years curriculum. Early years practitioners will have read advice on history with young children, talked to colleagues in their school and to colleagues in other schools, possibly through cluster group meetings on non-contact days. A lot of thinking, preferably collegial thinking, will have gone into identifying existing early years practices that can be maintained and extended with the new material. Similarly, attention will be given to innovative aspects of the history curriculum. How, for example, is the idea of primary sources (or evidence) to be treated? What about historical time? (Fortunately, there is sound, published guidance on these questions.) Does the curriculum imply new ways of working? How are they to be adopted and adapted? By whom and for whom? How does this vision fit our values?

The outcome of this interplay of formal study about history learning and teaching with collegial reflections upon experience and values is a version of national curriculum history that feels practicable. It is a set of provisional hypotheses, expressed in a plan of action. Action research into the implementation of these hypotheses will involve examining how well they run. The focus might be that general, or it might be more specific, expressed as a question such as: 'Is there enough scope for play in this topic?'

Practitioners might keep reflective logs, completed after each history session, recording what they felt about the sessions; what appeared to have gone well, and with whom; what seemed more problematic; and points to think about when re-planning the topic. Analysis of the logs might be done at the end of the topic (although it is likely that plans will also be modified as the topic proceeds in the light of reflections on each session). Typical questions will be whether the topic matched the plans, and whether divergence from those plans was beneficial or not (key national curriculum ideas got lost); whether the topic was too ambitious – and too ambitious for all children, or too ambitious for the practitioner, with limited supplies of energy; whether further modifications might allow for certain desirable early years practices to be more fully expressed in the topic, or for better links to be made with, say, number work; whether there are other ways of doing this – perhaps a whole-school 'blitz' on this topic once every three years might be better than doing it each year with just one age group? All of these questions are directed to generating new hypotheses in the shape of revised plans for future action.

Alternatively, each practitioner might talk with a colleague, who might be skilled in history, about a critical incident in each session, using the incident to tease out assumptions, routine practices, strengths and aspects of the plans that are being overshadowed by the demands of practice. Again, a session might be videotaped and then viewed first by the practitioner and then with a critical friend. Or children might form small groups and, rather like focus groups in market research, be interviewed about the work that they are doing – about what they know, understand, can do and feel. Again, practitioners might make time to stand back and look at what children *do* during this topic: Who talks with whom? Who appears to be engaged with the work? Who is apparently leading whom? What expressions have they on their faces (perhaps photos might be taken)? Where are they working? What sort of activities are they doing? Or children's work can be collected (always accepting that much valuable work is never in a form that can be collected) and the teacher might make a portfolio out of it to demonstrate to colleagues, or parents, what children had achieved in this topic. The portfolio would be a reference point for next year's planning. It would amount to research through the way that the practitioner selected work and accounted for that selection by explaining what it illustrated and what its significance was.

The outcomes of science work

A practical investigative, problem-working science topic is planned, much as with the history topic. Rather than address the process of teaching and learning, this piece of research follows the fashion of asking what difference has been made by it – what have children learned? Three approaches can be immediately identified. One asks what have children gained (a before–after model); a second asks whether they meet the pre-specified criteria of success (which may be the national curriculum statements of attainment); the third is open-ended, producing an account of children's science at the end of the topic, leaving it to the audience to decide what values to attach to the findings.

The before–after model depends upon having some measure of what children knew or could do before the topic, which is not easily obtained. Some practitioners use straightforward classroom talk as a way of gauging children's baseline knowledge, which is probably better than nothing. Focus groups or talk with individual children is to be preferred. In each case, there is an assumption that the practitioner raises questions based on the key ideas and skills that should be developed through the topic. Of course, where the topic is to develop skills or general ideas that have been encountered previously, information that has already been gathered in earlier work can provide the baseline.

The same methods can be used to establish what children know after the topic. Their work will also provide evidence of what they have understood and done. It is quite likely that the action researcher will find that children appear to be able to do more when judged against their classroom work than they do when judged on the basis of focus group sessions. The issue for practitioners is whether they are looking for evidence of perhaps fragile competence, of achievement in the security of the normal learning environment, or for evidence of more robust, partly generalized competence which can be displayed spontaneously out of context. It is helpful in such cases to be sure whether the task was teacher-led, teacher-supported or a consolidation task (see Chapter 3).

In the second case, the criteria of adequacy are set in advance, perhaps through the norms of statements of attainment. Seen like this, assessment within the national curriculum is potentially action research. Much has been written about the range of methods that may be used to assess children against national curriculum criteria, so we won't discuss methods of enquiry here. Instead, we take up a question that now becomes pressing: What is the difference between national curriculum teaching and action research? After all, both involve the systematic collection of evidence with a view to making a difference.

There is no necessary difference, save that action research involves raising values issues. Action research expects practitioners to wonder whether this is a good curriculum, whose interests are served by it and how it might be made better. Now, teachers of the under-fives have the freedom to follow these questions through to curriculum reform, but teachers of older children may raise these questions but can only act within the confines of the national curriculum – confines, it has to be said, that are frequently overestimated, especially given the changes presaged by the Dearing Report (1993). So while the methods of the national curriculum and of action research may coincide, the distinction between them lies not in the research part of the term, but in the action part.

The third approach to the outcomes of this science topic is wider-ranging than either of the others, hence closer to the spirit of action research. However, the scope for action is, of course, no less constrained. We might call this 'goal-free evaluation'. The action researcher is collecting evidence from any and all possible sources about the impact of the topic. That may involve looking at the impact on learning, as in the other two approaches, but it would be broader. The research might look, as in the history example, at the process of teaching and learning and make statements about the learning outcomes based upon it. For example, it might be that observation of children trying to join metals showed that they took up and held the idea that wet or shiny metals bonded, dull and dry ones didn't, all evidence to the contrary notwithstanding. Not only does this provide information about a learning outcome (the 'discovery' of shiny-ness rather than magnetism), but it also shows that another goal, discovery learning, needs to be reconceived, since it has led to wrong conclusions, presumably because the notion of 'fair testing' has been misunderstood as play, pure and simple. This directs our attention to the quality of the structuring that the teacher has provided for the activity. Goal-free evaluation could also probe children's feelings about this topic, estimate their levels of interest (were they similar among girls and boys?), perhaps ask parents too. And it would recognize that major outcomes of a topic are the effects it has on the practitioner, both emotional and educational.

In all three approaches to this science topic, we have seen methodological flexibility, a systematic approach to enquiry and a commitment to using the findings as the basis for change. Of course, the topic might have worked so well that it is not to be revised. Then the 'action' comes from applying the principles or lessons to another topic, to another group. Curriculum development, nevertheless, goes forward on the basis of the learning generated from these enquiries.

Action research and wider possibilities
Action research can be used as a way for practitioners to clarify and fulfil their educational values. Although this is not impossible within the years

covered by the national curriculum, those working with the under-fives have greater scope for developing curricula that embody their vision of education. In this section, we consider these wider research possibilities.

Activities might include:

1 Clarification of what parents want from the nursery, using question-naires, home visit interviews, meetings at playgroups and other social centres, involving parents further in curriculum creation, displays and presentations to parents, analysis of what does happen with children.
2 An examination of ways of providing more equal opportunities in edu-cation, which would involve getting data of all sorts to demonstrate the nature and extent of any existing inequalities, on the basis of children's age, social class, gender or race, and then planning, monitoring, evaluat-ing and changing a programme to try and ease the incidence of these inequalities.
3 Putting the year 2 curriculum – in its widest, post-Dearing sense – in a form that made for smoother transition into the junior school years of Key Stage 2, which would entail collaborative give and take with col-leagues teaching these older children and who often seem to hold rather different educational beliefs and to have rather different educational prac-tices; observation of each others' practices, sharing of thinking, ideals and constraints, as well as discussion with parents and children as they entered Key Stage 2.
4 Similar work to (3) on the transition into the reception year.
5 An attempt to improve the quality of children's 'free' time – dinner and play times (which for many children loom at least as large as the more formal schooling) – by examining what different children do at these times in different seasons, by talking with children, parents and those adults who supervise these sessions, by taking still or video photographs, by engaging children in design exercises to improve their play environ-ments, and by visiting other schools and talking with others.

Action research and other research

In each of these examples, practitioners have been depicted as acting in an intellectual vacuum, working only with their own resources and with data collected in the school setting. Yet these are not fresh topics, although they may well be fresh topics for *that* practitioner in *that* setting. Research and other reports exist and should be used within the action research cycle to do two things: one is to enrich practitioners' ideas about what is possible and at what price; the other is to suggest directions that may be more profitably pursued.

Action research and school-based curriculum development are sometimes described as 'rediscovering the wheel'. Our case has been that the key to curriculum development is the teacher as a learning and devel-oping person. That process involves the practical problem working that is action research, even if it does involve rediscovering the wheel: perhaps even if eight-sided wheels are discovered and tried out.

Yet we cannot take the position that it is the process of action research that matters, irrespective of the products. Some action research enthusiasts have taken that line, wrongly we believe, claiming for example that 'knowledge by definition cannot be in error' (McNiff 1993: 35) and that 'I do not believe that teachers "fail" within the terms of their own practice' (p. 51). There are three interlinked problems here. The first is that it is simply inefficient to claim that only the *process* of curriculum development and research matters. Besides, it is arguably immoral, since the aim of action research ought to be to do the best that is possible for children. The quality of the development *is* important, so curriculum development ought to tap into notions of best practice, contestable though they are. Second, not to refer to work by people who have worked on similar problems is irrational and hardly professional – almost arrogant. Third, as Desforges *et al.* (1986) argued, a major problem with action research is that practitioners often bring frameworks to bear upon it that are far too limited. Their work may suffer from seeing problems too narrowly, from failing to consider other perspectives and theories, and from not sufficiently questioning their own common sense. So Desforges and colleagues reported that teachers worried about overestimating the difficulty of work that children could do and were uninterested in the equally prevalent problem of underestimation. Similarly, work which we have already discussed on the place of academic subjects in early years education and on the future of the generalist classroom teacher raises possibilities that seldom enter into the reckoning in action research. The danger with action research as an attempt to work values through into practices, is that those values – existing beliefs about good early years practice – get taken for granted. Action research and curriculum development based on it may fail because they are lopsided: official values (i.e. those coming from 'above') may be criticized but practitioners' beliefs are taken for granted. Common sense – whatever that is – may become the new shibboleth.

Curriculum plans and an integrated model of curriculum development

Action research is the most promising tool that we have for curriculum development in the early years. However, its promise depends upon it not being precious and self-stroking. Moreover, this form of curriculum development is intensive, making demands upon practitioners such that swathes of the curriculum will remain untouched, even though this form of curriculum development is never-ending. Furthermore, since it arises from the problems felt by individual practitioners, it is unsystematic and somewhat unpredictable (Nias *et al.* 1992). So while valuing this approach to curriculum development, not least for its power to promote self-development and professional growth, we cannot see it as the only way of developing the curriculum.

A school needs to have a curriculum development plan for the next three to five years, annually updated and approved with governors. This will be the link between identifying areas for attention and the deployment of resources and the programme of professional development within the school. Ideally, it will relate to the school's statements of aims, although these statements are usually so bland and gargantuan in scope that they are practically useless.

The process of planning (which is discussed further in the next chapter) will say much about the sort of place that a school is. While we favour a process of review and learning that involves all adults working in the school, and which has heard parents, children and other educationists, we recognize that this collegiality and openness are not to everyone's taste. The plan ought, in any case, to draw upon some systematic reviews of present practice. We suggest that a basic curriculum audit be done. Once or twice a term teachers ought to identify the content that they are teaching, relating that to the building blocks of the curriculum, which we have taken to be academic subjects. At its crudest, schools should have some idea of how much time is spent on maths, English or art. Linked to that should be an analysis of the teaching and learning methods used. Alexander (1992) has argued that the national curriculum has had limited impact here and that the range used in Key Stage 2 is too limited. For preschool institutions, the question is whether the range matches the school's educational claims. It might be difficult to do this for a whole class, in which case it would be sensible to track the activities encountered by one or two children in a group. As far as possible, some estimate of the time spent on different curriculum content and on different activities ought to be attempted. Aggregated across the school, this information will reveal the main gaps and highlight redundancy. Following Chapter 2, we insist that some estimate ought to be made of children's happiness, as an expression of their sense of efficacy.

The plan will also react to analyses of assessment data. Shipman (1990) has emphasized that the education reforms of the late 1980s have placed assessment at the heart of schooling. Whether the data come from national tests at age seven or from teacher assessments that have been aligned with assessments in other schools, Shipman's point is that these data tell us a great deal about the effectiveness of the school – about areas of achievement and about areas where developments would be timely. As early years educators become more used to collecting more useful data about children's learning than has often been the case, curriculum development can be much more tightly linked to documented learning needs.

In drawing up curriculum development plans, it might be useful for schools to keep three, rather cynical points before them:

1 The existing curriculum is likely to be too narrow, both in terms of content and in terms of the balance of teaching and learning activities.
2 The curriculum for younger children is likely to be insufficiently demanding for some.
3 The curriculum in year 2 – perhaps year 1 also – is likely to be more formal than necessary.

Following the plan, we identify five levels of curriculum development, described below. We assume that teachers will be well-grounded in knowledge of child development and learning, as sketched in Chapters 1–3.

1 Maintain existing practice.
2 Raise awareness of other possibilities, content, resources and approaches: perhaps have practitioners working alongside each other; use a colleague as a 'beacon' making public elements of her interesting practice; introduce new information through meetings in non-contact time; be represented on relevant INSET courses.
3 Bring expertise into the school, perhaps by involving student teachers in a small development project; through a bespoke INSET session; through consultancy.
4 Support colleagues' individual curriculum development work through action research – seeking advice from the staff as a group and reporting back to them.
5 Undertake whole-school curriculum development, drawing upon action research practices, to tackle a school-wide issue (enhancing collaborative learning without pandering to bossy boys).

In early years institutions, teachers' work is wrapped up with the work of other adults, including parents, to a far greater degree than in schools in general. To a substantial extent, the creators of the curriculum for children will be adults other than teachers, although the professionals have responsibility for it. Consequently, it is essential that curriculum planning and development – and staff development – embrace all those who have relevant educational contact with the children. There is little point in teachers developing curriculum when other adults are creating it with children in counter-productive ways, simply because they do not know what else they should be doing, or fail to understand it or lack sufficient a repertoire to be able to do it. Since many of these adults are paid hourly or are volunteer colleagues, we recognize that there are difficult management issues in bringing them fully into curriculum planning, research and development.

Curriculum development for the early years is a complex mix of action research, more formal professional learning and institutionally co-ordinated learning. Clearly, then, success will not depend on individuals' enterprise alone, but will also reflect the extent to which the school is organized as a learning institution. It is to that we turn in the next chapter.

Points for reflection

1 The biggest problem with action research is getting people involved. What factors hinder colleagues from engaging in an action research approach to their work? How might the impact of these factors be reduced in your setting?

Further reading

We have already suggested a number of books that give useful introductions to action research methods (see p. 128).

DEVELOPING THE ORGANIZATION

The practitioner and the organization

The skill of practitioners as individuals is important for effective early years education. There is no doubt that children respond to different teachers, for instance, in different ways. Equally, there is a growing body of research showing that the school also makes a difference to children's learning. We suggest that the same is true for other educational organizations. Table 9.1 illustrates this.

Following our discussion of curriculum development, we stated that improvements in education are not just the result of improving individuals, by helping them to become action researchers for example. The organization within which they work has the ability to rob their efforts of their proper impact, to stifle the will to learn. It also has emergent properties. That is to say that in 'learning organizations' the efforts of individuals have collective impact that is greater than the sum of their separate contributions. Good organizational forms add value to people's work: poor ones steal it. In passing, we add that it is surprising that there has been so little research into the nature of effective institutions for early years education. Perhaps this reflects a misplaced belief that early years education is often on too small a scale and too informal to merit organizational analysis. We disagree, and think that research into effective organizational structures for early years learning is now the greatest priority.

The diversity of early years provision needs to be taken into account. Early years education takes place in a number of settings, apart from the home. Different settings have different priorities (compare day-care nurseries and nursery schools) and different organizational forms. Education gets different emphases and the facilities for education also differ from institution to institution. There are two ways of facing this: one is to

Table 9.1 Effective teachers and effective schools

	Effective teacher	Less effective teacher
Effective school	The ideal: the organization and the teacher reinforce each other	An effective school can carry this teacher and next year will, with luck, bring a fresh teacher
Less effective school	The trouble with this combination is that the teacher is working alone and next year is likely to be a worse year	A dreadful prospect!

respond to this diversity and treat the different forms of provision separately; the other is to claim that there are, nevertheless, certain common features of organizations that are geared to effective education, and to dwell on those. Since we have been looking in general at the ideas of education and curriculum as applied to young children, the second strategy is the one we prefer.

Bureaucracy and early years education

Bureaucracies are rule-governed, hierarchical organizations. They are often seen as lumbering, wrapped in red tape and impersonal. These characteristics would be considerable faults in any organization dedicated to early years education, especially as people and interpersonal relationships lie at the heart of educational effectiveness. However, some aspects of early years education do need to be put on a bureaucratic basis. Our concern is that playgroups, nurseries, schools and day centres may be regarded as small organizations which run through informal, daily personal contact, with the result that structural, recurring and systematic matters can get overlooked. We are not saying that playgroups should become bureaucracies. What we are saying is that all educational establishments have bureaucratic concerns. Effective educational establishments have structures that are flexible while ensuring that priorities and routines are put into practice. This blend of tightness and flexibility is a characteristic of professional and effective organizations. For example, procedures-with-flexibility are needed in the following cases:

◀ *Systems for liaising with other organizations.* Everyone agrees that liaising with the social and health services is important and the Children Act (Department of Health 1989) emphasizes that. However, it must not –

as the Children Act implies – be left to informal, individual actions. Policies, procedures and agreements are needed (Pugh 1993). In the same way, liaison with other education and care facilities is needed, particularly in order to manage well children's *and* parents' transitions from one place to another. At the very least, a full review of existing practices is needed in order to ask whether it is wide-ranging enough and of sufficient quality. Children and parents will be involved in this review.

◀ We have discussed *parent-professional relationships*. Some aspects of these relationships also need to be put on a bureaucratic basis, in the sense that rules and routines will ensure that all homes are given the same minimum service. That does not, of course, mean that contacts have to be bureaucratic, grim and grudging in nature. Nor does it prevent greater contacts from occurring. It simply defines an entitlement for all homes, saying when, where and by whom it is to be worked through.

◀ In maintained and independent schools, *governing bodies* have considerable rights and authority. Often seen as a burden on the profession, governing bodies can greatly contribute to a school's well-being. Local education authorities have run many governor training courses on governors' responsibilities, publicizing good working routines. Schools also need to be professional in working with governors and in being accountable to them. This demands bureaucratic procedures as well as good, personal working relationships.

The Children Act has bureaucratic expectations of providers of education for the under-fives and of day care for the under-eights. For example:

◀ provision for children with special needs;
◀ the promotion of equal opportunities;
◀ health issues;
◀ policy on modifying children's unacceptable behaviour;
◀ premises and space standards.

Likewise, the Rumbold Report (DES 1990a) said that places educating three- and four-year-olds ought to have, among other things:

◀ a policy outlining aims and objectives, based upon a clear philosophy;
◀ a policy on quality control (it would be better to devise a total quality management policy);
◀ a clear management structure;
◀ record-keeping;
◀ a staff development plan.

All of these requirements may be described as bureaucratic, although their existence *does not* make schools and nurseries into bureaucracies. Indeed, it is highly desirable that such policies and procedures are drawn up collegially. Once in place, there needs to be regular, systematic monitoring to see that they are functioning and with what effects.

The concept of review is familiar within schools and some nurseries. They have to present annual institutional development plans to their governing bodies. Increasingly, within schools these plans are being developed on the basis of curriculum review and analysis. The Guidelines for School Review and Development (GRIDS: Abbott *et al.* 1988) provide a useful impetus for review and planning. Interestingly, the GRIDS system incorporates many of the action research principles we outlined in Chapter 8.

Reviews of early years education provision need to be sensitive to the special nature of the phase and its different providers. Early in a review it is helpful to work from a checklist, but checklists detailing what is seen as important in good-quality provision need to be regarded simply as scaffolding. Commercially produced checklists will miss things that are important to you and your colleagues and stress things that may not be your current, main concerns.

A well-regarded list, to which we referred in Chapter 6, is the *Early Childhood Environment Rating Scale* (Harms and Clifford 1980). It is designed for evaluating preschool provision. It has seven categories and the scale as a whole is said to be reliable, which means that it is quite robust as an assessment device. The categories are:

1 Furnishings and display for children, which includes provision of basic materials.
2 Language-reasoning activities, which examine the range of language materials in a classroom, the provision of planned language activities, and the planned introduction and development of concepts.
3 Fine and gross motor activities. This 1980 scale did not mention computer and console use as a way of developing fine motor coordination.
4 Creative activities, including provision for art, music, movement, block, sand, water and dramatic play.
5 Social development, including provision of space to be alone, as well as for free play, always with regard to 'cultural awareness' and the tone of interpersonal relationships.
6 Personal care routines, focusing on the provision of meals and snacks, toilets, and personal grooming.
7 Adult needs – the provision of space for adults, including parents, and the extent of opportunities for professional growth.

While commending this approach to organizational review, we must repeat that the checklist is simply a starting point. Indeed, this much-used list does not do justice to the ways of learning that we have valued in Chapters 2 and 3, nor to the curriculum breadth that we described in Chapter 6. Ideally, groups of providers would take this or a similar scale as a starting point and go on to customize their own checklist that reflected their own priorities and their own organizational structures.

Such a customized, flexible, bureaucratic system is also needed for staff appraisal and for the regular supervision sessions that operate in the day-care sector. Appraisal and supervision are useful ways of recognizing what colleagues do well and of planning for continuing professional learning. Appraisal is particularly important as a way of identifying what an organization is doing well and where there are gaps. As such, appraisal ought to feed through to an institution's development plan.

The bureaucratic features of the organization and its goals are important, because they together describe many of the tasks that need to be done and which might otherwise not be done, or done in part only. We know that it is hard to find time for such management tasks. Colleagues who feel that they never have time to manage properly may be consoled by the following list, which describes features of management work in commercial, business and other non-education settings.

◀ frenetic
◀ fragmented – brief spells of activity, often interrupted
◀ concerned with *ad hoc*, day-to-day matters
◀ concrete, concerned with practicalities rather than abstractions
◀ reactive
◀ eclectic
◀ interactive
◀ improvised, with decisions and plans being developed while the manager is in the middle of a problem (after Hales 1993: 14).

Yet there are dangers in analysing organizations in terms of procedures alone, for we end up with a set of flow charts and requirements that describe a peopleless place.

Processes: people and effective organizations

Whether you look at the literature on commercial organizations (Peters and Waterman 1983; Peters 1990; Drucker 1993), at the literature on quality assurance (Murgatroyd and Morgan 1993) or at the literature on education management (Rosenholtz 1991; Nias *et al.* 1992; Whitaker 1993; Hargreaves 1994), there is agreement that effectiveness is related to the way people feel, to what they value, to how they relate to each other as humans, and to how they learn at work. It is important that structures, policies and routines exist as a context for this human interaction, but it is also certain that the quality of what happens within identical systems varies a great deal and distinguishes the effective from the less effective institution. As Mortimore and colleagues (1988: 262) said of effective junior schools: 'The twelve key factors point to effective schools as being friendly, supportive environments . . . an effective school has a positive ethos'. The Rumbold Report similarly pointed to the importance of 'an atmosphere in which every child and adult feels secure, valued and confident' (DES 1990a: 35).

The quality of relationships within an organization affects more than just the way in which it runs. It also affects the way in which it changes.

Fullan (1991), summarizing many writings on educational change, has concluded that changing schools is about changing people. Change depends on practitioners altering their beliefs, adding to or changing their knowledge, and revising their practices and routines. Change, then, like the learning it involves, is very personal and can be very threatening. The most effective change is likely to happen in environments where the quality of relationships is good enough to reduce people's feelings of threat; where people feel that colleagues will support them; where people expect to learn professionally; and where people expect to take risks because they know that schooling is too complicated for there to be risk-free, straightforward solutions to the practical issues that face them.

This is the major task of the leader of an organization, be it a small playgroup or a large infant school – to lead (most definitely) in ways that support people in risk-taking, in tinkering with the curriculum, in problem working and in reflecting. The effective leader is not 'a scolding presence, a direct threat to [teachers'] sense of self worth' (Rosenholtz 1991: 56), although he or she will sometimes criticize. The effective leader helps people to grow, by setting an example and by promoting the characteristics which we shall shortly discuss – collegiality, rather than servility, for example. We will not examine here ways in which people learn to lead, although we do believe that it is something that many can do.

Leaders need not just be the senior person in an organization. Anyone can lead and the view that we take of effective organizations is that everyone should have the chance to lead colleagues in some venture at some times. For example, a nursery nurse might be dissatisfied with the ways in which children relate to each other and, consulting with colleagues, work regularly with a group of children in order to try and get them to think about other people's feelings as well as their own. This, incidentally, involves ignoring the common, but wrong belief that this is something that young children cannot do. Her methods appear to work and are spread through the wider group of children. Subsequently, she shares her work at a staff meeting and works with other interested colleagues. As such, she is leading, not so much by being *in* authority but more because she is *an* authority on this topic.

Nias and colleagues (1992) said that much whole-school curriculum development takes this form, spreading out from the work which one or two practitioners did as they tinkered with the curriculum. It is slow but it is well-adapted to the setting, flexible, influential and on a human scale. Owned by the practitioners, rather than imposed from above, it is also satisfying. This shows us that change comes from below as well as from above. Both sorts of change depend upon the organization being people-friendly. Thence it can become innovation-friendly.

People-friendly collegiality is not enough, though. It is a necessary part of institutional change but it is not a sufficient condition of change. Without the commitment to professional learning, this friendliness can lead to nothing more than comfy stagnation. The message is that effective early years learning is related to clear bureaucratic practices, developmental planning, and to good interpersonal relationships and to a commitment to learning of the sort that we described in the last chapter. We will now list five human attributes of effective schools, beginning with a commitment to professional learning.

A learning culture

Nursing currently seems to be establishing itself as a profession. One of the major obstacles to this process is the hostility of many nurses to 'the clever nurse' (Mackay 1990). This anti-intellectualism makes it difficult to take forward the claim that nursing is a profession, since the main characteristic of a profession is that it trades in a specialist knowledge that lay people lack. Within the teaching profession, practitioners' professional learning is therefore crucially important, as specialist knowledge has to be constantly developed and fine-tuned to the demands of different contexts. In the last chapter we argued that, professionally speaking, a learning culture is important to early years practitioners. It follows that learning needs to be built into the organization so that it is truly a learning organization.

Hawkins and Shohet (1989) have identified some features of a learning culture which we have summarized as:

◄ learning and development are seen as life-long processes;
◄ all work situations are seen a potential sites for learning, as are problems and even crises;
◄ learning is an interplay between theory, planning and actions;
◄ part of a manager's job is to ask how other practitioners might be helped to maximize their learning;
◄ there is feedback to individuals and teams;
◄ the organization is flexible, with shifting roles and responsibilities on the understanding that learning is part of everyone's work together.

This fits with Hargreaves' (1994) view that organizations adapted to our 'post-modern world' will be 'moving mosaics'. By this he means that boundaries between my work and yours are constructively blurred, so that we each have our own responsibilities while also having shared interests and activities. Moreover, our roles will change over time, rather than being fixed, so that stimuli for learning are limited. Figure 9.1 illustrates this and other organizational forms.

The sketches in Fig. 9.1 show how people relate to each other. We are assuming that bureaucratic procedures operate to set the tasks that have to be done and to say who is responsible for doing them and when. We are not here offering any comment on those procedures, except to say that in (b) the procedures focus on the headteacher, (represented by the shaded block) whereas in (d) different tasks will involve different people (represented by the unshaded blocks) in different ways at different times. Figure 9.1 (a) shows an organization that is, almost literally, atomized. That in (b)

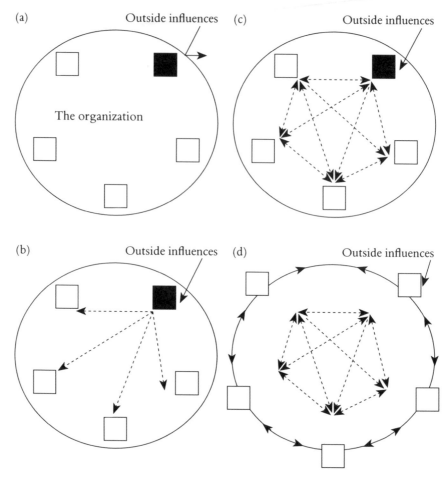

Figure 9.1 Models of professional relationships

is hierarchical. In (c), the organization is collegial, although roles are fixed, to the degree that the headteacher remains in place. In the 'moving mosaic' represented by (d), jobs rotate. This organization is also shown as being directly accessible to outsiders. Here,

> warm human relationships of mutual respect and understanding, combined with the toleration and even encouragement of debate, discussion and disagreement create flexibility, risk-taking and continuous improvement among the staff which in turn lead to positive results among the students and positive attitudes among the staff to changes and innovations which might benefit those students.
>
> (Hargreaves 1994: 239)

Or, to use Rosenholtz' (1991: 214) words, 'the successful school is . . . where teaching professionals are asked to make reflection and its requisites the master of action and its requisites'.

A culture
A culture has been described as '. . . the collection of traditions, values, policies, beliefs and attitudes that constitute a pervasive context for everything we do and think in an organization' (McLean and Marshall 1983, cited in Hawkins and Shohet 1989: 133). In effective organizations there is a high degree of consensus about goals. One of the most important things a new recruit to a staff team learns about is the values and beliefs that distinguish the place, in both their official and unofficial forms.

What is the source of this culture, ethos, atmosphere or sense of purpose? History is one source. The way people have talked, behaved and interacted in the past and its consequences give every organization a cultural form. As we have suggested, that form may not be too conducive to effectiveness, as if the past lay drowsily upon the present, soothing away any will to think differently.

Another source of organizational culture is the leader, usually in the shape of the senior person. Just about the most important part of their job is thought to be building a culture that is conducive to effectiveness. For that to happen, leaders need a vision of what effective early years education looks like, in terms of its content, of ways of working, and of the organizational forms that promote effectiveness. Their job is the complex one of patiently modelling the vision, encouraging colleagues to work in ways that are consistent with it, prompting reviews and policies to promote it, and accepting that cultures take years to evolve and that they evolve at an uneven pace. This vision, worked out with governors and staff into an increasingly confident policy, will be the linchpin of the organization's set of stated aims or mission statement. Schools are now expected to plan with their mission statements in mind and they are to be assessed and inspected on that basis.

A common piece of advice is that leaders should concentrate on areas in which progress is most likely to be made, working particularly through colleagues sympathetic to the emerging vision. They should also give ground on non-essentials, accepting that their vision must be modified by colleagues as those practitioners come to feel an ownership of it.

But is this not giving too much importance to philosophical issues that are far removed from the daily business of educating young children? We think not, for two reasons. The first is that some parts of this vision of a culture, or ethos – notably those concerning the ways in which adults are to relate to each other and to their work – are absolutely crucial to the effectiveness of the organization. A hierarchical and status-riddled school is going to be a very different place to a 'moving mosaic': it will attract different staff, respond to children and parents in a different way, and innovate, we predict, through changes on the surface only. There is an interesting parallel here with themes which we developed in Chapter 2. Just as children need to have their self-esteem preserved, if not enhanced, and to feel effective and capable as learners, so too with practitioners. Where this 'empowerment' is lacking, where practitioners feel neither valued nor able to change things, then disillusion, boredom and obstructiveness creep in. The institution ceases to be a learning institution and gets 'stuck' (Rosenholtz 1991).

The second reason why the culture of an organization is important is because children deserve continuity of treatment. A fragmented school teaches children different things in different ways at different points. Their learning lacks coherence, continuity and progression. It is also likely to lack breadth and balance. A common culture tends to lead to learning in one year that builds upon learning that has taken place in earlier years and that leads through to next year's as well. Children get consistent messages about how to behave to each other, coupled with consistent attempts to encourage their self-esteem and a sense of educational worthiness.

Collegiality

'Collaboration is not, however, a panacea which will heal all divided staff groups', Nias and colleagues (1992: 149) remind us. Nonetheless, collegiality and collaboration are valued as ways of encouraging professional learning, of strengthening the organizational culture, of developing the organization, and of providing mutual support. Hargreaves (1994) has listed eleven potential benefits to practitioners of collaboration and organizations. Nias *et al.* (1994: 271–2) summarized the value of a 'culture of collaboration' thus:

> Its existence made it possible for headteachers, teachers and ancillaries routinely and unselfconsciously to work as a team, that is, to behave, despite all their differences, as if they shared a common goal, to feel collectively responsible for its attainment, and always be ready to help one another towards it. It was this culture which helped staff members, including the head, to identify as a group, that is to see one another as friends and to feel a satisfying sense of social cohesion . . . Shared understandings and agreed behaviours enable staff in schools where this culture is dominant to trust and to learn from one another. ·

Yet collaborative cultures are also voluntary, partly informal and unpredictable. Bureaucratic needs for *this* to be done *now* may not fit well with a collegial preference to concentrate on other things, to assert that the ways that things have been done so far are quite adequate, or to prefer other values to those in the official line. Collegiality is desirable, but it does not necessarily lead to effective education. That depends on the cultural context and on the commitment to learning that go with the collegiality. It also depends on structures and agreements that permit intentions to be taken forward into actions. Roles and responsibilities may change, as in the moving mosaic model of relationships, but it is important that they are known and that they are filled. There is a difference between a moving mosaic and smoke patterns on the wind. The former has a pattern and a purpose; the latter is chaos.

Self-understanding

Implicit in this idea of collegiality is the belief that effective educators have a personal maturity about them. Working collegially means giving something of ourselves to others and accepting that their beliefs and practices will differ from ours *and* that we will have to give ground just as much as we expect to get others to come closer to our thinking. It is scary. It involves having a sense of self-worth that is so strong that it does not need to be strident.

So, for example, potential competition and rivalry among early years workers is sometimes made worse by the status differences between nursery nurses, teachers and classroom assistants. Just acknowledging that is a step away from letting it become harmful. More important still is being clear about how you feel about differences with colleagues, and why, and with what justification. Often, differences are about trivia – small organizations can be fertile ground for petty-mindedness – and represent insecurities and faulty self-knowledge. Differences that matter and matters of indifference can get gloriously entangled, damaging the organization in the process. Leaders certainly need skill at interpersonal understanding but practitioners also need to look inwards.

Promising work has been done with teachers who are encouraged to look at the ways they *feel* about teaching, relating their work to their lives and to their own biographies. It can help people to become clearer about why they work and think as they do, to examine the implications of going about things differently and to be more confident about their own identities. And perhaps it is confident humility that is the key to effective organizations: confidence in one's identity and sense of self – as a teacher and as a person – allied to the humility and tentativeness that recognize that there is much to learn and many ways of doing things that are worth taking seriously.

Few of us are such paragons, but that does not lessen the value of this vision. Effective organizations value bureaucratic practices, but those routines are only scaffolding within which personal relationships and sense of self are worked out.

Points for reflection

1 What aspects of your work need to be covered by rules and routines? Which parts definitely should be exempt from such bureaucratic attentions? Why? Bear in mind that you may be a paragon but colleagues may need more structure to their work.

2 How collegial is your workplace? Could collegiality be enhanced, and if so, how? What benefits might you realistically expect to come from greater collegiality?

Further reading

As we have said, these issues have not been directly addressed in research into early years education. On school management in general, we recommend Whitaker (1993). Rosenholtz's (1991) research into Tennessee elementary schools gives a very human account of effective schools, while Mortimore and colleagues' book (1988) is the classic British work.

10 ⬦ ENDPIECE

We have offered a complex account of effective early years education. If we want to *educate* young children, rather than preside over their development, then such complexity cannot be avoided. Education is a moral, hence a complex and contested activity.

It also demands knowledge. We have taken a broad view of the knowledge that is needed. We are particularly in sympathy with Bruner's (1966) view that to avoid trivializing the educational enterprise, educators should attend to knowledge about children's development, knowledge about how to teach and knowledge about knowledge. Others have paid much more attention to knowledge of child development and implied that this was sufficient for effective early years education. We emphatically reject that. Knowledge of child development is necessary but it is nothing like sufficient. Hence, we have shown early years practice as an area with a rich and demanding knowledge base. The need for knowledge about instruction and knowledge about knowledge leads us to emphasize the importance of practitioners in children's learning.

We have also tried to be sensitive to some of the differences in practice between those working with the under-fives and those working with older children. We find Wood's (1988) description of the difference a helpful one. He sees the role of those working with very young children to be one of *capturing* the learning opportunity in situations of spontaneity. By highlighting aspects of an event, adults can bring children to useful ways of understanding. Teachers of older children have to *recruit* children to tasks that will develop their understanding. The vast differences for learners in expectations, behaviour, power and control between capture and recruitment demonstrates for us the enormous demands made on reception class teachers in the British education system. Managing this learning transition is extremely difficult, but crucial.

We have argued that early years educators should be regarded as professionals. We believe that mastery of the relevant knowledge base is a necessary condition if an occupation is to be ranked as a profession. Another element is decision making. We have argued that even where the national curriculum operates, practitioners are faced with a host of decisions at different levels of their work. Collectively, there are decisions to be negotiated about the values and aims of the organization in which learning occurs. Curriculum, in the sense of content and ways of working, has to be planned. (We reject the view that the national curriculum has necessarily stripped this important work from teachers, although it has redefined its scope.) Other school policies, about work with parents for example, have to be created. Decisions about learning tasks have to be made and the consequences of those decisions have to be evaluated in terms of their effect on children's learning and on their sense of self-worth. And the whole web of decisions needs to be subject to the professional analysis that is at least rigorous reflection and at its most detailed is action research.

We recognize a danger that this account may seem to emphasize rational planning and neglect the important contributions of experience, flexibility and opportunities for spontaneity and use of the imagination. However, that is not our intention. As we have said, classrooms are complex places, often 'on the edge of chaos'. That phrase is carefully chosen, since some scientists believe that creativity and innovation are maximized at the edge of chaos. The term is not derogatory. But because classrooms are so often on the edge of chaos, there has to be a place for spontaneity and intuition. We also know very well how chaotic young children can be. Yet one feature of the edge of chaos is that it is organized. Without wanting to ignore the unpredictable, and without denying the sheer exuberance of young children, we want to insist that to work to best effect in these conditions requires a deliberate, knowledgeable and intelligent cast of mind. It needs professionals.

REFERENCES

AAHPERD (1991). Physical education and health education in early childhood. In D. Elkind (ed.), *Perspectives on Early Childhood Education*. Washington, DC: National Education Association.

Abbott, R., Steadman, S. and Birchenough, M. (1988). *GRIDS Primary School Handbook*, 2nd edn. York: Longman.

Ainscow, M. (1991). *Effective Schools for All*. London: David Fulton.

Alexander, R. (1984). *Primary Teaching*. London: Cassell.

Alexander, R. (1992). *Policy and Practice in Primary Education*. London: Cassell.

Alexander, R., Rose, J. and Woodhead, C. (1992). *Curriculum Organisation and Classroom Practice in Primary Schools*. London: Department of Education and Science.

Anderson, C.W. and Smith, E.L. (1987). Teaching science. In V. Richardson-Koehler (ed.), *Educators' Handbook*, pp. 84–111. New York: Longman.

Anning, A. (1991). *The First Years at School*. Buckingham: Open University Press.

Apple, M.W. (1982). *Education and Power*. London: Routledge and Kegan Paul.

Aspland, R. and Brown, G. (1993). Keeping teaching professional. In D. Bridges and T. Kerry (eds), *Developing Teachers Professionally*, pp. 6–22. London: Cassell.

Aubrey, C. (ed.) (1994). *The Role of Subject Knowledge in the Early Years of Schooling*. London: Falmer Press.

Barnes, J. (1986). *Staring at the Sun*. London: Cape.

Becher, J. (ed.) (1994). *Governments and Professional Education*. Buckingham: SRHE/ Open University Press.

Bennett, N. and Carré, C. (eds) (1993). *Learning to Teach*. London: Routledge.

Bennett, N. and Cass, A. (1988). The effects of group composition or group inter-active processes and pupil understanding. *British Educational Research Journal*, **15**(1): 19–40.

Bennett, N. and Dunne, E. (1992). *Managing Classroom Groups*. Hemel Hempstead: Simon and Schuster.

Bennett, N., Desforges, C., Cockburn, A. and Wilkinson, B. (1984). *The Quality of Pupil Learning Experiences*. Hove: Lawrence Erlbaum Associates Ltd.

Bereiter, C. (1972). Schools without education. *Harvard Education Review*, **42**(3): 390–413.

Bernstein, B. (1971). *Class Codes and Control*, Vol. 1. London: Routledge and Kegan Paul.

Blank, M. (1973). *Teaching and Learning in the Preschool*. Columbus, OH: Charles E. Merrill.

Blatchford, P. (1990). Pre-school reading skills and later reading achievement. *British Education Research Journal*, **16**(4): 425–8.

Blatchford, P. (1991). Children's writing at seven years. *British Journal of Educational Psychology*, **63**: 73–84.

Breedlove, C. and Schweinhart, L.J. (1982). *The Cost Effectiveness of High Quality Early Childhood Programs*. Report for 1982 Southern Governors Conference. Ypsilanti, MI: High Scope Press.

Brown, A. (1993). Participation, dialogue and the reproduction of social inequalities. In R. Merttens and J. Vass (eds), *Partnerships in Maths: Parents and Schools*, pp. 190–213. London: Falmer Press.

Browne, N. (ed.) (1991). *Science and Technology in the Early Years*. Buckingham: Open University Press.

Bruner, J.S. (1960). *The Process of Education*. Cambridge, MA: Harvard University Press.

Bruner, J.S. (1966). *Towards a Theory of Instruction*. Cambridge, MA: Harvard University Press.

Bruner, J.S. (1974). *Relevance of Education*. Harmondsworth: Penguin.

Bruner, J.S. (1983). *Child's Talk*. Oxford: Oxford University Press.

Bullock, A. (1975). *A Language for Life*. London: HMSO.

Burns, R.B. (1982). *Self-concept Development and Education*. London: Holt, Rinehart and Winston.

Burrage, M. and Torstendahl, R. (eds) (1990). *Professions in Theory and History: Rethinking the Study of Professions*. London: Sage.

CACE (1967). *Children and their Primary Schools* (The Plowden Report). London: HMSO.

Campbell, R.J. (ed.) (1993). *Breadth and Balance in the Primary Curriculum*. London: Falmer Press.

Campbell, R.J. and Neill, S.R.St.J. (1994). The use of primary teachers' time: Some implications for beginning teachers. In J. Bourne (ed.), *Thinking Through Primary Practice*. London: Routledge.

Campbell, R.J. *et al.* (1992). The changing world of infant teachers. *British Journal of Education Studies*, **40**(2): 149–62.

Carraher, T., Carraher, D. and Schliemann, A. (1990). Mathematics in streets and in schools. In P. Light, S. Sheldon and M. Woodhead (eds), *Learning to Think*, pp. 231–5. Milton Keynes: Open University Press.

Catling, S. (1990). Early mapwork: Mapwork with 5 to 8 year olds. In *Primary Geography Matters*. Sheffield: The Geographical Association.

Chambers, J.H. (1990). Forms of knowledge, the curriculum and the young child. *Early Child Development and Care*, **61**: 51–6.

Cockcroft, W. (1982). *Mathematics Counts*. London: HMSO.

Curtis, A. (1986). *A Curriculum for Pre-school*. Windsor: NFER/Nelson.

David, T., Curtis, A. and Siraj-Blatchford, I. (1992). *Effective Learning in the Early Years*. Coventry: University of Warwick.

Dearing, R. (1993). *The National Curriculum and its Assessment*. London: HMSO.

Department of Education and Science (1990a). *Starting with Quality*. London: HMSO.
Department of Education and Science (1990b). *Technology in the National Curriculum*. London: HMSO.
Department of Education and Science (1990c). *English in the National Curriculum*. London: HMSO.
Department of Education and Science (1992a). *Art in the National Curriculum*. London: HMSO.
Department of Education and Science (1992b). *Music in the National Curriculum*. London: HMSO.
Department of Education and Science (1992c). *PE in the National Curriculum*. London: HMSO.
Department of Health (1989). *The Children Act 1989: Guidance and Regulations*. London: HMSO.
Desforges, C. (1985). Matching Tasks to Children's Attainment. In N. Bennett and C. Desforges (eds), *Recent Advances in Classroom Research*, pp. 92–104. Edinburgh: Scottish Academic Press.
Desforges, C. (ed.) (1989). *Early Childhood Education*. Edinburgh: Scottish Academic Press.
Desforges, C.W. and Cockburn, A. (1987). *Understanding the Mathematics Teacher*. Lewes: Falmer Press.
Desforges, C.W., Cockburn, A. and Bennett, N. (1986). Teachers' perspectives on matching: implications for action research. In D. Hustler, T. Cassidy and T. Cuft (eds), *Action Research in Classrooms and Schools*, pp. 67–72. London: Allen and Unwin.
Donaldson, M. (1978). *Children's Minds*. Glasgow: Fontana/Collins.
Doyle, N. (1983). Academic work. *Review of Educational Research*, **53**: 159–200.
Doyle, W. (1986). Classroom Organization and Management. In M.C. Wittrock (ed.), *Handbook of Research on Teaching*, 3rd edn. New York: Macmillan.
Drucker, P. (1993). *Post-capitalist Society*. London: Butterworth-Heinemann.
Dunn, J. (1988). *The Beginnings of Social Understanding*. Oxford: Blackwell.
Early Years Curriculum Group (1989). *Early Childhood Education: The Early Years Curriculum and the National Curriculum*. Stoke on Trent: Trentham Books.
Edwards, A. (1984). The development of self in the preschool child. Unpublished PhD thesis, University of Wales.
Edwards, A. (in press). The curriculum applications of classroom groups. In P. Kutnick and C. Rogers (eds), *Groups in Schools*. London: Cassell.
Edwards, A. and Talbot, R. (1994). *The Hard-pressed Researcher: A Handbook for the Caring Professions*. London: Longman.
Edwards, D. and Mercer, N. (1987). *Common Knowledge: The Development of Understanding in the Classroom*. London: Methuen.
Elliott, J. (1991). *Action Research for Educational Change*. Buckingham: Open University Press.
Feasey, R. (1993). Scientific investigation. In R. Sherrington (ed.), *Science Teachers' Handbook*. Hemel Hempstead: Simon and Schuster.
Floyd, A. (1981). *Developing Mathematical Thinking*. London: Addison Wesley/Open University Press.
Fontana, D. and Edwards, A. (1985). Teachers' preceptions of socio-economic development in nursery school children. *The Durham and Newcastle Research Review*, October, pp. 239–42.

Froufe, J. (1990). Influences on children's performance. *Questions*, January, pp. 18–21.

Fullan, M. (1991). *The New Meaning of Educational Change*. London: Cassell.

Gardner, H. (1983). *Frames of Mind: The Theory of Multiple Intelligences*. New York: Basic Books.

Hales, C. (1993). *Managing Through Organisation*. London: Routledge.

Hall, N. and Abbott, L. (1991). *Play in the Primary Curriculum*. London: Hodder and Stoughton.

Hannon, P. (1989). How should parental involvement in the teaching of reading be evaluated? *British Journal of Educational Research*, **15**(1): 33–40.

Hannon, P. and James, S. (1990). Parents' and teachers' perceptives on preschool literacy development. *British Educational Research Journal*, **16**(3): 259–72.

Hargreaves, A. (1994). *Changing Teachers, Changing Times*. London: Cassell.

Harlen, W. (1993). Children's learning in science. In R. Sherrington (ed.), *Science Teachers' Handbook*, pp. 37–54. Hemel Hempstead: Simon and Schuster.

Harms, T. and Clifford, R.M. (1980). *Early Childhood Environment Rating Scheme*. New York: Teachers' College Press.

Harré, R. (1983). *Personal Being*. Oxford: Blackwell.

Hartley, D. (1993). *Understanding the Nursery School*. London: Cassell.

Hawkins, P. and Shohet, P. (1989). *Supervision in the Helping Professions*. Buckingham: Open University Press.

Hegarty, S. (1987). *Meeting Special Needs in Ordinary Schools*. London: Cassell.

Henriques, J., Holloway, W., Urwin, C., Venn, C. and Walkerdine, V. (1984). *Changing the Subject*. London: Macmillan.

Hitchcock, G. and Hughes, D. (1989). *Research and the Teacher*. London: Routledge.

HMI (1990). *The Teaching and Learning of Reading in Primary Schools*. London: DES.

HMI (1991). *Standards in Education 1989–90*. London: DES.

Honess, T. and Edwards, A. (1987). Evaluative and case study research with adolescents. In T. Honess and K. Yardley (eds), *Self and Identity: Perspectives Across the Lifespan*, pp. 246–61. London: Routledge.

Hopkins, D. (1993). *A Teacher's Guide to Classroom Research*, 2nd edn. Buckingham: Open University Press.

Hughes, M. (1986). *Children and Number*. Oxford: Blackwell.

Hughes, M., Wikely, F. and Nash, T. (1993). Parents in the new era: Myth and reality. In R. Merttens and J. Vass (eds), *Partnerships in Maths: Parents and Schools*, pp. 103–12. London: Falmer Press.

Hurst, V. (1991). *Planning for Early Learning*. London: Paul Chapman.

Hurst, V. (1993). *Early Years Education in Jeopardy*. London: Early Years Curriculum Group.

James, W. (1890). *Principles of Psychology*. New York: Holt.

Jones, A. and Mercer, N. (1993). Theories of learning and information technology. In P. Scrimshaw (ed.), *Language, Classrooms and Computers*, pp. 11–26. London: Routledge.

Kagan, S.L. and Zigler, E.F. (1987). *Early Years Schooling: The National Debate*. New York: Yale University Press.

Kellmer-Pringle, M. (1980). *The Needs of Children*, 2nd edn. London: Hutchinson.

Kellogg, R. (1979). *Children's Drawing, Children's Minds*. New York: Avon Books.

Kelly, V. and Blenkin, G. (1993). Never mind the quality, feel breadth. In R.J. Campbell (ed.), *Breadth and Balance in the Primary Curriculum*. London: Falmer Press.

Kerry, T. and Sands, M. (1992). *Handling Classroom Groups: A Teaching Skills Workbook*. London: Macmillan.

Knight, P. (1987). Children's understanding of people in the past. Unpublished PhD thesis, Lancaster University.

Knight, P. (1991). *History at Key Stages One and Two*. York: Longman.

Knight, P. (1992). Myth and legend at Key Stage One. *Primary Education Review*, **6**(3, 4): 237–44.

Knight, P.T. (1993). *Primary Geography, Primary History*. London: David Fulton.

Knight, P. and Smith, L. (1989). In search of good practice. *Journal of Curriculum Studies*, **21**(5): 427–40.

Lally, M. (1991). *The Nursery Teacher in Action*. London: Paul Chapman.

Loenen, A. (1989). The effectiveness of volunteer reading help and the nature of the reading help provided in practice. *British Journal of Educational Research*, **15**(3): 297–316.

Mackay, L. (1990). Nursing: Just another job? In P. Abbott and C. Wallace (eds), *The Sociology of the Caring Professions*, pp. 29–39. London: Falmer Press.

McKernan, J. (1991). *Curriculum Action Research*. London: Kogan Page.

McNamara, D. (1994). *Classroom Pedagogy and Primary Practice*. London: Routledge.

McNiff, J. (1993). *Teaching as Learning*. London: Routledge.

Mead, G.H. (1934). *Mind, Self and Society*. Chicago, IL: University of Chicago Press.

Merttens, R. and Vass, J. (1990). *Bringing School Home: Children and Parents Learning Together*. London: Hodder and Stoughton.

Merttens, R. and Vass, J. (eds) (1993). *Partnerships in Maths*. London: Falmer Press.

Milner, D. (1983). *Children and Race Ten Years On*. London: Ward Lock.

Mortimore, P. *et al.* (1988). *School Matters*. Wells: Open Books.

Munn, P. (1992). Teaching strategies in nursery settings. Paper presened to the *Education Section of the British Psychological Society Annual Conference*, Wokingham, November.

Murgatroyd, S. and Morgan, C. (1992). *Total Quality Management and the School*. Buckingham: Open University Press.

NAEYC/NAECSSDE (1991). Guidelines for appropriate curriculum content and assessment in programs serving children ages 3 through 8. *Young Children*, **46**(3): 21–38.

Nias, J., Southworth, G. and Campbell, P. (1992). *Whole School Curriculum Development in the Primary School*. London: Falmer Press.

Nias, J., Southworth, G. and Yeomans, R. (1994). The culture of collaboration. In A. Pollard and J. Bourne (eds), *Teaching and Learning in the Primary School*, pp. 258–72. London: Routledge.

Nisbet, J. and Shucksmith, J. (1986). *Learning Strategies*. London: Routledge and Kegan Paul.

Norman, D. (1978). Notes towards a complex theory of learning. In A.M. Lesgold, J.W. Pollegrino, S.D. Fokkema and R. Glaser (eds), *Cognitive Psychology and Instruction*. New York: Plenum Press.

Peters, T. (1990). *Thriving on Chaos: Handbook for a Management Revolution*. London: Pan.

Peters, T. and Waterman, R.H. (1983). *In Search of Excellence*. New York: Harper and Row.

Phillips, T. (1985). Beyond lipservice: Discourse development after the age of nine. In G. Wells and J. Nicholls (eds), *Language and Learning: An Instructional Perspective*. London: Falmer Press.

Pugh, G. (1987). Introduction. In G. Pugh, G. Aplin, E. De'Ath and M. Moxon, *Partnerships in Action*, Vol. 1. London: National Children's Bureau.

Pugh, G. (ed.) (1993). *Contemporary Issues in the Early Years*. London: Paul Chapman.

Rogers, C. (1989). Early admission: Early labelling. In C. Desforges (ed.), *Early Childhood Education*, pp. 94–109. Edinburgh: Scottish Academic Press.

Rosenholtz, S.J. (1991). *Teachers' Workplace*. New York: Longman.

Sammons, P., Nuttall, D. and Cuttance, P. (1993). Differential school effectiveness: Results from a reanalysis of the ILEA's Junior School Project. *British Educational Research Journal*, **19**(4): 381–405.

Sedgwick, D. and Sedgwick, F. (1993). *Drawing to Learn*. London: Hodder and Stoughton.

Shayer, M. and Adey, P. (1981). *Towards a Science of Science Teaching*. London: Heinemann.

Shipman, M. (1990). *In Search of Learning*. Oxford: Blackwell.

Shuard, H. (1986). *Primary Mathematics Today and Tomorrow*. York: Longman.

Solomon, Y. (1989). *The Practice of Mathematics*. London: Routledge.

Spodek, B. and Saracho, O.N. (1990). Early childhood curriculum construction and classroom practice. *Early Child Development and Care*, **61**: 1–9.

Sylva, K., Siraj-Blatchford, I. and Johnson, S. (1992). The impact of the UK national curriculum on pre-school practice. *International Journal of Early Childhood*, **24**(1): 41–51.

Taylor, C. (1977). What is human agency? In T. Mischel (ed.), *The Self: Psychological and Philosophical Issues*, pp. 103–35. Oxford: Blackwell.

Taylor, W. (1994). Teacher Education: Backstage to Centre Stage. In T. Becher (ed.), *Governments and Professional Education*. Buckingham: SRHE/Open University Press.

Tizard, B., Mortimore, J. and Burchell, B. (1981). *Involving Parents in Nursery and Infant Schools*. London: Grant McIntyre.

Tizard, B. and Hughes, M. (1984). *Young Children Learning*. London: Fontana.

Tizard, B. *et al.* (1988). *Young Children at School in the Inner City*. Hove: Lawrence Erlbaum Associates Ltd.

Topping, K. and Wolfendale, S. (eds) (1985). *Parental Involvement in Children's Reading*. London: Croom Helm.

Torstendhal, R. and Burrage, M. (ed.) (1990). *The Formation of Professions: Knowledge, State and Strategy*. London: Sage.

Tough, J. (1976). *The Development of Meaning: A Study of Children's Use of Language*. London: Allen and Unwin.

Vincent, C. (1993). Community participation? The establishment of a 'City Parents' Centre'. *British Educational Research Journal*, **19**(3): 227–41.

Vygotsky, L.S. (1978). *Mind in Society*. Cambridge: Harvard University Press.

Wade, B. (1992). Reading recovery: Myth and reality. *British Journal of Special Education*, **19**(2): 48–51.

Walden, R. and Walkerdine, V. (1982). *Girls and Mathematics: the Early Years*. Bedford Way Paper No. 8. London: Institute of Education.

Walden, R. and Walkerdine, V. (1985). *Girls and Mathematics: From Primary to Secondary Schooling*. Bedford Way Paper No. 24. London: Institute of Education.

Walkerdine, V. (1988). *The Mastery of Reason*. London: Routledge.

Waterland, E. (1988). *Read with Me*, 2nd edn. Stroud: Thimble Press.

Wells, G. (1981). *Learning Through Interaction*. Cambridge: Cambridge University Press.

Wells, G. (1986). *The Meaning Makers*. London: Hodder and Stoughton.

Whitaker, P. (1993). *Managing Change in Schools*. Buckingham: Open University Press.

Willes, M. (1983). *Children into Pupils*. London: Routledge and Kegan Paul.

Wittrock, M. (ed.) (1986). *Handbook of Research on Teaching*. New York: Macmillan.

Wood, D. (1986). Aspects of teaching and learning. In M. Richards and P. Light (eds), *Children of Social Worlds*, pp. 191–212. Cambridge: Polity Press.

Wood, D. (1988). *How Children Think and Learn*. Oxford: Blackwell.

Wright, A. (1992). Evaluation of the first British Reading Recovery Programme. *British Educational Research Journal*, **18**(4): 351–68.

INDEX

QUALITY EDUCATION IN THE EARLY YEARS
Lesley Abbott and Rosemary Rodger (eds)

Lesley Abbott and her team of contributors identify and explore high quality work (and what shapes it) in early years education. They show us children and adults variously working and playing, talking and communicating, learning and laughing, caring and sharing in a rich tapestry of case studies which highlight quality experiences and interactions. Every chapter is based around a particular case study, each one tackling a different issue: the curriculum, play, assessment, roles and relationships, special needs, partnerships with parents, and equal opportunities.

All the writers work together in early years education on a day-to-day basis enabling them to pool their different expertise to create a balanced but challenging approach. They give inspiring examples of, and outline underlying principles for, quality work and ask important questions of all those involved in the education and care of young children.

Contents
Introduction: The search for quality in the early years – A quality curriculum in the early years: Raising some questions – 'Play is fun, but it's hard work too': The search for quality play in the early years – 'Why involve me?' Encouraging children and their parents to participate in the assessment process – 'It's nice here now': Managing young children's behaviour – 'She'll have a go at anything': Towards an equal opportunities policy – 'We only speak English here, don't we?' Supporting language development in a multilingual context – 'People matter': The role of adults in providing a quality learning environment for the early years – 'You feel like you belong': Establishing partnerships between parents and educators – 'Look at me – I'm only two': Educare for the under threes: The importance of early experience – Looking to the future: Concluding comments – Bibliography – Index.

Contributors
Lesley Abbott, Janet Ackers, Janice Adams, Caroline Barratt-Pugh, Brenda Griffin, Chris Marsh, Sylvia Phillips, Rosemary Rodger, Helen Strahan.

224pp   0 335 19230 0 (Paperback)   0 335 19231 9 (Hardback)

THE EXCELLENCE OF PLAY

Janet R. Moyles (ed.)

Child: When I play with my friends we have lots of fun . . . do lots of things . . . think about stuff . . . and . . . well . . .
Adult: Do you think you learn anything?
Child: Heaps and heaps – not like about sums and books and things . . . um . . . like . . . well . . . like *real* things.

Anyone who has observed play for any length of time will recognize that, for young children, play is a tool for learning. Professionals who understand, acknowledge, and appreciate this can, through provision, interaction and intervention in children's play, ensure progression, differentiation and relevance in the curriculum.

The Excellence of Play gathers together authoritative contributors to provide a wide-ranging and key source text reflecting both up-to-date research and current classroom practice. It tackles how we conceptualize play, how we 'place' it in the classroom, how we relate it to the curriculum, and how we evaluate its role in learning in the early years. It will stimulate and inform debate through its powerful argument that 'a curriculum which sanctions and utilizes play is more likely to provide well-balanced citizens of the future as well as happier children in the present'.

Contents

Introduction – Part 1: The culture of play and childhood – Play and the uses of play – Play in different cultures and different childhoods – Sex-differentiated play experiences and children's choices – Play, the playground and the culture of childhood – Part 2: Play, schooling and responsibilities – Play and the legislated curriculum. Bach to basics: an alternative view – 'Play is ace!' Developing play in schools and classrooms – Fantasy play: a case for adult intervention – Making play work in the classroom – Part 3: Play and the early years curriculum – Play, literacy and the role of the teacher – Experiential learning in play and art – Bulbs, buzzers and batteries: play and science – Mathematics and play – Part 4: Assessing and evaluating play – Evaluating and improving the quality of play – Observing play in early childhood – Play, the universe and everything! – Afterword – References – Index.

Contributors

Lesley Abbott, Angela Anning, Tony Bertram, David Brown, Tina Bruce, Audrey Curtis, Rose Griffiths, Nigel Hall, Peter Heaslip, Jane Hislam, Victoria Hurst, Neil Kitson, Janet R. Moyles, Christine Pascal, Roy Prentice, Jeni Riley, Jane Savage, Peter K. Smith.

240pp   0 335 19068 5 (Paperback)   0 335 19069 3 (Hardback)

THE FIRST YEARS AT SCHOOL
EDUCATION 4 TO 8

Angela Anning

This is a practical and reflective discussion of the education of 4 to 8 year-olds based on a sympathetic recognition of the complexities of being an early years teacher. Angela Anning begins by reviewing the historical and ideological traditions of British infant and primary schools, tracing how we have reached the position where teachers are torn between child-centred progressivism and utilitarian demands in educating young children. She then provides a detailed and authoritative critique of accepted thinking about the cognitive, social and emotional development of children; and explores the complexities of teachers' roles, particularly in the areas of language, intervention and expectations. She discusses the organization of the classroom, the structuring of learning in the school day and the content of the curriculum. She tackles the implications of the National Curriculum and national assessment for seven year-olds and their impact on pre-fives and children with special educational needs.

The book is filled with practice-based knowledge about the curriculum, children, and teaching and learning. As such it should commend itself to all who have an interest in promoting quality education through the management, planning, teaching and assessment of the curriculum for 4–8 year-olds in the 1990s and beyond.

(Christopher Day)

Contents
Histories and ideologies – Children learning – Teachers teaching – The curriculum – A National Curriculum for 4–8 year-olds – Into the new ERA – References – Name index – Subject index.

168pp   0 335 09592 5 (Paperback)   0 335 09593 3 (Hardback)